TOP **10**

SAN FRANCISCO

CONTENTS

SAN FRANCISCO

INTRODUCING

The Transamerica Pyramid in Downtown

WELCOME TO
SAN FRANCISCO

From the Golden Gate Bridge to the Painted Ladies, delicious dim sum to vintage cable cars, San Francisco is a nonstop feast for the senses. Don't want to miss a thing? With Top 10 San Francisco, you'll enjoy the very best the city has to offer.

San Francisco has inspired writers, artists, filmmakers, and chefs – and it's easy to see why. Full to bursting with sprawling parks, world-class museums, emerging cuisines, and historic neighborhoods, the City by the Bay is loaded with sights and experiences sure to impress visitors.

The best way to see all that San Francisco has to offer is by simply wandering the city's steep streets, with the engineering marvel that is the Golden Gate Bridge serving as a constant backdrop. Along the way, spot cable cars crawling up the city's hills, take a detour into the stunning

A cable car traveling the streets

parks of the Presidio and Golden Gate, and admire the pastel facades of the Victorian Painted Ladies.

But San Francisco's icons aren't limited to the outdoors. Visit the city's museums and you'll find an abundance of treasures, from the incredible textile collections of the de Young to the jaw-dropping art on display at SFMOMA. And the dining options are endless, from mouth-watering dishes like Burmese tea leaf salad to photo-worthy dumplings.

While the city's highlights are beyond a doubt, don't overlook its understated gems. These can be experienced by boutique-shopping in the Mission District or by heading into Fillmore clubs to catch some live jazz. There are also diverse and buzzy neighborhoods to explore, from the historic African American Arts and Culture District in Bayview to the food- and karaoke-filled Japantown. And there's plenty to discover beyond the city's outskirts, too, including Napa Valley and its 400-plus wineries, the redwood trees of Muir Woods, and the Bay Area's student scene.

So, where to start? With Top 10 San Francisco, of course. This pocket-sized guide gets to the heart of the city with simple lists of 10, expert local knowledge and comprehensive maps, helping you turn an ordinary trip into an extraordinary one.

THE STORY OF
SAN FRANCISCO

San Francisco began when the Ramaytush Ohlone arrived 1,500 years ago. Waves of changemakers have washed up on its foggy shores since – Spanish missionaries, Gold Rush miners, counterculture hippies, and tech titans – transforming the city. Here's the story of how it came to be.

The Ohlone canoeing in San Francisco Bay

San Francisco Begins

The indigenous Ramaytush Ohlone arrived in San Francisco in 500 CE, naming the settlement and surrounding area Yelamu. When Spanish colonists arrived here in 1769, they named the settlement Yerba Buena ("good herb") after a native plant similar to mint. Under orders of the Spanish crown, the colonists established the Presidio of San Francisco in 1776 to gain a foothold in northern California, founding the mission of San Francisco de Asís (the Spanish name for Saint Francis of Assisi) nearby. But following Mexico's independence from Spain in 1821, Mexico then claimed the area as part of its territory. The official name change to "San Francisco" happened in 1847. In 1848, the Treaty of Guadalupe Hidalgo ended the two-year border dispute of the Mexican-American War, and Mexico ceded land to the United States, including all of what is now California.

A painting showing ships in San Francisco Bay during the 1840s

A depiction of gold miners in San Francisco

Gold Rush to Exclusion

The discovery of gold in the Sacramento Valley sparked the California Gold Rush of 1849, attracting prospectors (known as "49ers") from around the world. Prosperity followed, helping to usher in California's statehood in 1850. The pioneering Transcontinental Railroad also broke ground in Sacramento, 87 miles (140 km) north of San Francisco, in 1863. Together with the Gold Rush, the railroad attracted Chinese laborers, and it was racism toward these workers – they were paid less than their white counterparts, for example – that led to the creation of the city's Chinatown, the first in the US. Other ethnic enclaves followed, providing safe spaces for hitherto persecuted communities.

White workers, including immigrants fleeing famine in Ireland, and white legislators felt threatened by the Chinese presence and successfully passed the Chinese Exclusion Act of 1882. This severely restricted new immigration from China and was the first law of its kind to discriminate based on country of origin. It wasn't formally repealed until 1943.

Moments in History

500 CE
The Ramaytush Ohlone Indigenous peoples are the first settlers in what is now San Francisco; they came to use the area's abundant resources.

1776
Spanish colonists establish the Presidio of San Francisco as part of the "New Kingdom of Spain" to gain a foothold in northern California.

1848
The Treaty of Guadalupe Hidalgo ends the Mexican-American War, and Mexico cedes all of California to the US.

1849
The California Gold Rush begins and San Francisco rapidly expands from a tiny hamlet into a boomtown.

1882
The Chinese Exclusion Act halts Chinese immigration as growing numbers of Chinese laborers compete with white men for decreasing amounts of gold.

1968
Students organize one of the longest US student strikes, in support of the civil rights movement. It reinforces the ideal of the city as a hub for social justice.

1981
The devastating disease later known as AIDS is first detected in San Francisco; the ensuing epidemic sees the launch of the San Francisco AIDS Foundation.

1995
The dot-com bubble brings an influx of tech workers and drives up the local cost of living; its burst leads to a recession.

2020
The COVID19 pandemic spurs retail and tech companies to leave the city.

2023
Revitalization efforts led by Mayor London Breed begin and include housing small businesses in vacant office spaces and new night markets. The program is called Vacant to Vibrant.

Earthquake and Rebuilding
Disaster struck San Francisco on the morning of April 18, 1906, when a huge earthquake ruptured the San Andreas fault, killing over 3,000 people and destroying more than 80 percent of the city. San Francisco was rebuilt in a few years, only to be devastated again economically by The Great Depression from 1929 to 1939. However, its participation in the Depression-era Works Progress Administration led to the construction of the iconic Golden Gate Bridge, completed in 1937.

World War II to the 1980s
During World War II, the government uprooted and incarcerated Japanese Americans in 1942, dissolving the city's Japantown. At the same time, Black shipyard workers arrived as part of the Great Migration out of the post-slavery South, forming communities near the shipyard and in the spaces formerly occupied by Japanese Americans – in the Fillmore, the immigration sparked an arts renaissance that nicknamed it the "Harlem of the West."

After, as the Vietnam War waged and the civil rights era began in the 1960s,

The aftermath of the 1906 earthquake

San Francisco's Union Square at dusk

the Third World Liberation Front, a movement spearheaded by students at San Francisco State University and UC Berkeley, resulted in the birth of Ethnic Studies and Asian American Studies. In conjunction with Oakland's Black Panther movement, the Mexican and Filipino United Farm Workers' unionization in the Central Valley, the hippie counterculture's Summer of Love, anti-Vietnam War activism, and second-wave feminism, this era cemented San Francisco's status as a hub of social justice.

The catastrophic 1980s AIDS epidemic hit the city's sizable queer population, but some important legacies of it were the San Francisco AIDS Foundation and the AIDS Memorial Grove in Golden Gate Park.

San Francisco Today

Following the Loma Prieta earthquake of 1989, which once again took lives and destroyed parts of the city, the late 1990s ushered in the first dot-com boom, when US tech firms based in Silicon Valley, just south of San Francisco, grew very powerful, very quickly. With the influx of well-paid tech workers to the city, neighborhoods like the Mission saw gentrification and cost-of-living increases. After the tech bubble burst in 2000, many of these companies went out of business, which was then followed by an era of executive scandals and recession.

But then, within the next decade, major tech companies such as Twitter (X) and Uber were founded and headquartered in San Francisco, and while the pandemic of the early 2020s caused large companies to once again leave the city, emerging tech sectors such as artificial intelligence (AI) still gravitate toward the Bay Area.

Efforts to revitalize the city following the pandemic have begun, including a small-business incubation program that places local vendors in empty downtown office spaces, while new parks and night markets are popping up, from the Mission to North Beach. San Francisco is also now home to several cultural districts, an effort to pay homage to the city's diverse and storied heritage, from the mural-filled Calle 24 Latino Cultural District in the Mission to the Tenderoin's Transgender District, the first of its kind in the world. With these steps, San Francisco continues to be a city of resilience and acceptance, and one that welcomes visitors with open arms.

TOP 10
EXPERIENCES

Planning the perfect trip to San Francisco? Whether you're visiting for the first time or making a return trip, there are some things you simply shouldn't miss out on. To make the most of your time – and to enjoy the very best this city has to offer – be sure to add these experiences to your list.

1 Picnic at the Presidio
This beautiful park *(p104)* is perfect for a relaxing day out, with highlights including a close-up view of the Golden Gate Bridge, an education center full of interesting info, and a playground made of upcycled materials. Treat yourself to a scenic picnic, taking advantage of the Presidio's wide array of food trucks.

2 Explore the city's cultural districts
San Francisco has ten cultural districts, each one dedicated to a neighborhood's unique history. From the American Indian Cultural District in the Mission *(p116)*, to the Leather and LGBTQ Cultural District in SoMa *(p115)*, they're perfect for exploring the city's vibrant history.

3 Dig into dim sum
From casual takeout to upscale sit-down, feasting on dim sum is a must in the city. San Francisco's Chinatown *(p32)* is the largest outside Asia and the oldest in North America. Walk its historical streets filled with restaurants and sample their delicious soup dumplings, rice noodle rolls, and pork buns.

4 Join the festive fun
San Francisco knows how to have fun, and its huge range of festivals shows the city's many faces. Celebrate the Lunar New Year at the US's largest festival *(p88)*, join the crowds at the renowned Pride Parade *(p88)*, or indulge in some foot-stomping at the Stern Grove Festival *(p89)* summer concerts.

5 **Hike the Crosstown Trail**
Want to see the city in a different light? The volunteer-led Crosstown Trail traverses the city with paths that you can walk, run, or cycle. Along the way, you'll visit local neighborhoods less frequented by tourists, such as Bernal Heights and Visitacion Valley.

6 **Delight in urban wildlife**
San Francisco has an unexpected menagerie of charismatic creatures. Head to PIER 39 *(p26)* to visit the lively sea lion colony, keep an eye out for parrots on Telegraph Hill *(p98)*, and watch the American bison graze in Golden Gate Park *(p36)*.

7 **Enjoy a beach sunset**
With west-facing views across the ocean, there's no better place to watch the sunset than on San Francisco's beaches. Head to East Beach *(p67)* for a view of the Golden Gate Bridge, or visit the Pacifica Beaches *(p66)* to watch surfers and explore nature trails.

8 **Sample the Bay Area's bounty**
Thanks to the Bay Area's fertile fields and ample waters, there's no limit to fresh produce. The Ferry Plaza Farmers Market *(p82)* on Saturdays features more than 100 vendors, and there are plenty of markets throughout the week.

9 **Visit world-class museums**
From modern art at SFMOMA *(p42)* to Claude the albino alligator at CalAcademy *(p39)* to cutting-edge costume collections at the de Young *(p40)*, San Francisco's museums illustrate just how much culture and science is on offer in this small city.

10 **Root for San Francisco's home teams**
Cheer on the Golden State Warriors and Golden State Valkyries at the Chase Center, or catch a fly ball at a San Francisco Giants game at Oracle Park *(p102)*. The venues are huge, the fans are serious, and the food is delicious.

ITINERARIES

Exploring Alcatraz Island, eating dim sum in Chinatown, visiting the SFMOMA: there's a lot to see and do in San Francisco. With places to eat, drink, or simply take in the view, these itineraries offer ways to spend 2 days and 4 days in the city.

2 DAYS

Day 1

Morning
Start the day in SoMa with a cardamom-infused coffee and pastry at Yemeni coffee shop Sana'a Cafe *(p121)*. Walk a few minutes southwest to SFMOMA *(p42)*, one of the largest museums of modern and contemporary art in the US, to take in the exhibitions such as Alexander Calder's hanging mobiles and Yayoi Kusama's immersive and colorful mirror rooms. End your visit with a coffee on the museum's rooftop at Cafe 5 before browsing the eclectic offerings in the ground-level gift shop.

Afternoon
Walk 20 minutes north to Chinatown *(p32)* or take the Muni metro to

Digging in to Tony's pizza outside

 DRINK
A requisite drink initiation for San Francisco visitors, Buena Vista *(p107)* in Fisherman's Wharf whips up thousands of original hot Irish coffees, punched up with Irish whiskey, sweet sugar, and lightly whipped fresh cream.

Chinatown-Rose Park station, which has several site-specific artworks by local artists. Grab a dim sum lunch at the historic Hang Ah Tea Room *(hangahdimsumsf.com)*, the first one of its kind in the US. Once you've had your fill of dumplings and buns, explore the sights in America's oldest Chinatown, including a dedicated Bruce Lee exhibit at the Chinese Historical Society of America *(p33)* and Chinese diasporic art at the Chinese Culture Center *(p33)*. After, head west to the nearby North Beach neighborhood for Beatnik history, browsing the City Lights Bookstore *(p98)* which was founded in 1953 by Lawrence Ferlinghetti, who famously published and supported Beat poets and writers. Enjoy a pizza slice at Tony's *(p97)* for dinner and converse with locals at Vesuvio *(p100)*.

Day 2

Morning
Take in the morning Bay water views and and then head inside the Ferry Building *(p52)* on the Embarcadero for

Walking the paths at the Presidio Tunnel Tops

artisanal eats and boutiques. A great breakfast here is a guava *malasada* from Ocean Malasada (*oceanmalasada.com*) and a Mission Mocha from Dandelion Chocolate (*dandelionchocolate.com*). If it's a Tuesday, Thursday, or Saturday, you can also browse the Ferry Plaza Farmers Market just outside. After, ride a vintage F-Market streetcar north and hop off to visit the hands-on Exploratorium (*p95*). Then continue north to the must-see areas of Fisherman's Wharf (*p26*) and PIER 39 (*p26*), catching the sea lions frolicking on the pier.

Afternoon
Make your way west to Ghirardelli Square (*p83*) for an early afternoon sweet treat at the Chocolate Experience.

The square is also a great dining spot for something more savory for lunch; try the Detroit-style pizza at Square Pie Guys (*squarepieguys.com*). Walk or take the 30 bus to the Presidio Tunnel Tops park (*p104*), for an evening stroll capturing snaps of the Golden Gate Bridge. Have a relaxing sunset dinner overlooking the ocean at one of the park's many food trucks.

> **VIEW**
> A ride on the F-Market streetcar allows for views of some of the city's most iconic buildings. As you travel, spot the Asian Art Museum (*p56*), Opera House (*p97*), and Symphony Hall (*p97*).

Map labels:

Presidio Tunnel Tops Park
3
Presidio
PRESIDIO
GO SHUTTLE
Baker Beach
Lobos Valley
Lands End
Sutro Baths
Seal Rock Inn Restaurant
Safeway
RICHMOND
Rise & Grind 4
Golden Gate Park
Ocean Beach
Saigon Sandwich
Japan Town
Fillmore
WESTERN ADDITION
City Hall
HAYES VALLEY
CIVIC CENTER
Nopa
Alamo Square Park
Main Library
HAIGHT ASHBURY
LOWER HAIGHT
MISSION
Amoeba Music
Grateful Dead House
GLBT Historical Society Museum
Rainbow Honor Walk
Roxie Theater
Dumpling Kitchen

4 DAYS

Day 1

Kick-start your stay in San Francisco with a coffee from Blue Bottle (p77) and an empanada from El Porteño (elporteno.com) at the Ferry Building (p52). Hop on a ferry for a quick ride to Treasure Island (p103), built in 1939 for the Golden Gate Exposition. From here, take in the views from the Cityside Park and visit the photo archives at the

EAT
The imposing Mission-style burritos (p74) — filled with rice, beans, cheese, pico de gallo, avocado, and protein — were invented in San Francisco and illustrate the city's Chicano history. Try ones from El Farolito (p121).

Treasure Island museum (treasure islandmuseum.org). Then, tuck into lunch in the a beautiful garden setting at Aracely Cafe (aracelysf.com). After journeying back to the Ferry Building, hop on another ferry to Alcatraz Island (p28) and once there, tour the former prison. Make sure to use the audio guide – it's included with every ferry ticket. Time your return to catch the sunset and have dinner at Codmother (p107).

Day 2

Eat breakfast at the Saluhall at the Downtown IKEA (p83), then go half a

The Ferry Building at Embarcadero

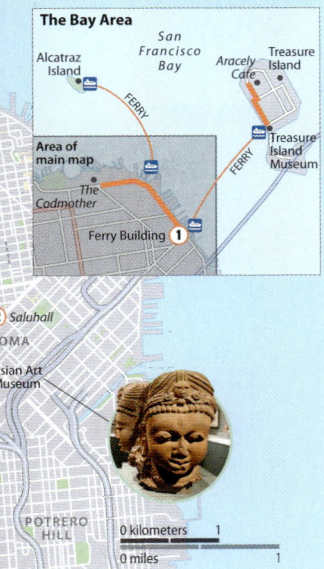

The Bay Area

Alcatraz Island

San Francisco Bay

Aracely Cafe

Treasure Island

Treasure Island Museum

Area of main map

The Codmother

Ferry Building **1**

2 Saluhall

SOMA

Asian Art Museum

POTRERO HILL

0 kilometers   1

0 miles   1

---

mile southwest to the Beaux Arts-style Civic Center *(p97)*, where you can check out free exhibits at the Main Library, explore the displays at the Asian Art Museum, and marvel at the gold- and marble-accented City Hall. Have a casual late lunch at Saigon Sandwich *(saigon-sandwich-sf.com)*. Walk west, passing through Japantown and the Fillmore, and then south to Alamo Square Park to see the famous Painted Ladies *(p111)*. End the day with dinner at the ever-popular Nopa *(p113)*.

Day 3

Begin the day in the rolling hills of Presidio Tunnel Tops park *(p104)* where you can grab a pastry at the Mess Hall *(messhallpresidio.com)*. Ride the free Presidio GO Shuttle west to Baker Beach *(p66)* and relax on the sand with views of the Golden Gate Bridge. Next, head to the entrance of Lands End *(p123)*, then hike 80 minutes along the coastal bluffs for views of the ocean, shipwrecks, and what remains of the Sutro Baths *(p71)*, ending on Point Lobos Ave to refuel at the Seal Rock Inn Restaurant *(p151)*. If

it's burn season (Mar–Oct), buy firewood and snacks nearby and head to Ocean Beach *(p123)* to build a campfire; if not, take the time to enjoy the sunset at the beach with locals.

Day 4

Start your last day at Rise & Grind *(rise andgrind-sf.com)* in the Inner Richmond for a latte and breakfast sandwich. Make your way into Golden Gate Park *(p36)* to marvel at exotic plants in the Conservatory of Flowers, before going south to Haight-Ashbury *(p111)*, visiting neighborhood gems like Amoeba Music *(p112)* and the Grateful Dead house, where the band lived in the 1960s. For lunch, go south to Dumpling Kitchen *(dumplingkitchenca.com)* in the Castro, home of some of the city's best dim sum. After you've filled up, visit the nearby GLBT Historical Society Museum *(p57)* and the Rainbow Honor Walk to learn about the city's LGBTQ+ history. Come evening, catch an indie flick at the Roxie Theater *(roxie.com)* then grab a Mission-style burrito *(p74)* from a neighborhood taqueria and spend the night bar-hopping around the Castro.

The Roxie Theater in the Castro

TOP 10 HIGHLIGHTS

The famous Fisherman's Wharf sign

EXPLORE THE
HIGHLIGHTS

There are some sights in San Francisco you simply shouldn't miss, and it's these attractions that make the Top 10. Discover what makes each one a must-see on the following pages.

1.5 miles (2 km) ❹

Sonoma ❿ Napa
Novato
San Rafael
Vallejo
Berkeley
Oakland
SAN FRANCISCO

0 km 20
0 miles 20

MARINA BLVD

JEFFERSON STREET

MARINA DISTRICT

BAY STREET

LOMBARD STREET

RUSSIAN HILL

COLUMBUS AVENUE

NORTH BEACH

VAN NESS AVENUE

TAYLOR STREET

COW HOLLOW

BROADWAY

❺

PACIFIC HEIGHTS

FINANCIAL DISTRICT

Alta Plaza

❷

❸

HAYES VALLEY

❾

3RD STREET

OAK STREET

Buena Vista Park

CASTRO STREET

CASTRO

❶ Golden Gate Bridge

❷ Cable Cars

❸ Fisherman's Wharf

❹ Alcatraz Island

❺ Chinatown

❻ Golden Gate Park

❼ California Academy of Sciences

❽ de Young Museum

❾ San Francisco Museum of Modern Art (SFMOMA)

❿ Wine Country

GOLDEN GATE BRIDGE

📍 C1 🌐 goldengate.org 📷

The immense scale of San Francisco's most iconic landmark is breath-taking. The bridge that many people said could never be built – the span was too wide, the ocean too deep, and the cost too high – opened in 1937. To experience this impressive structure first-hand, travel across it by foot, bike, bus, or car. For another perspective, head to one of the nearby viewpoints on the shore, or take a cruise to see it from the water.

1 Deco Style
The bridge owes its style to the consulting architect Irving F. Morrow. He simplified the pedestrian railings to uniform posts placed far enough apart to allow for unobstructed, scenic views.

Fort Point Lookout under the Golden Gate Bridge

2 Toll System
Since 1937, cars have been required to pay a toll to cross the bridge. Today, only city-bound traffic is charged, and since 2013, the fully automated electronic system allows vehicles to pass the toll point without stopping.

3 Maintenance
Repairing the bridge is an ongoing task and it's repainted continuously; the famous "International Orange" paint protects it from the salt in the air.

4 Fort Point Lookout
This National Historic Site *(p53)* was completed in 1861. It offers soaring views of the underside of the bridge and of the pounding waters beneath.

5 Marin Vista Point
Crossing over to the north side, pull off just before the end to take in the panorama from the Vista Point. Look back at the hills and spires of the city.

6 Presidio Tunnel Tops
Opened in 2022, the Presidio Tunnel Tops

Golden Gate Bridge towering above the Bay

TOP TIP

Chech sfcityguides.org for details about the free walking tours on Sundays and Thursdays.

park *(p104)*, near the Golden Gate Bridge, features many scenic overlooks that offer stunning views of the famous structure.

7 Bridge Celebrations

Since its opening on May 27, 1937, the bridge has been central to the city's soul, and is the setting for everything, from 4th of July fireworks to political demonstrations.

8 Star Turns in Movies

The bridge has starred in many movies, including Alfred Hitchcock's *Vertigo*, where James Stewart pulls Kim Novak from the surf near Fort Point *(p53)*. In *A View to a Kill*, 007 and Christopher Walken engage in a dramatic battle at its heights.

9 Cruises

For a unique view of the bridge, take a cruise around the Bay. There are various options to choose from. Daily sightseeing trips run by Red and White Fleet *(p143)* leave directly from Fisherman's Wharf and pass directly under the bridge. Hornblower Cruises *(p102)* depart from Pier 3 on the Embarcadero and offer tours that include brunch or dinner.

10 Hiking and Biking

The bridge is open to walkers and cyclists. Urban hiking trails and extensive cycle routes can be found on both sides of the bridge, in the Presidio and along the Marin Headlands.

THE STATISTICS

The length of the steel wires used to make the cables of the bridge is enough to circle the earth three times. It is said to be five times stronger than it needs to be to withstand the winds and tides it endures daily. At the time it was built, it was the longest suspension bridge in the world (it now ranks twelfth). About 40 million vehicles cross the bridge annually, streaming across six lanes of traffic, along its 1.7-mile (2.7-km) length. The bridge is equipped with two foghorns, each with a different pitch, and 360-degree flashing red beacons.

CABLE CARS

It's impossible not to love these vestiges of another age, as they make their way up the city's steep hills. Cable cars came close to being scrapped in 1947, when attempts were made to replace them with buses. However, after a public outcry, the present three lines, covering 10 miles (16 km), were retained, and the system was declared a National Historic Landmark in 1964.

TOP TIP

To skip the long lines at a terminal, walk up one or two stops, and hop on right away.

1 Cars
Cable cars come in two types: one that has a turnaround system, one that does not. All of them are numbered, have wood-and-brass fittings in the 19th-century style, and are often painted in differing colors. One car can accommodate around 60 to 70 passengers.

2 Grip Person
The grip person must be quick-thinking and strong to operate the heavy gripping levers and braking mechanisms. The grip acts like huge pliers that clamp onto the cable to pull the car along.

3 Bell
While operating up and down the hills, the cable car's bell is used by the grip person like a klaxon, to warn other vehicles and pedestrians of imminent stops, starts, and turns.

4 Braking
Cable cars have three different brakes. Wheel brakes press against the wheels; track brakes press against the tracks when the grip person pulls a lever; the emergency brake is a steel wedge forced into the rail slot.

CABLE CARS AND STREETCARS

Andrew Hallidie's cable car system dates from August 2, 1873, when he tested his prototype based on mining cars. It was an immediate success and spawned imitators in more than a dozen cities worldwide. However, 20 years later, it was set to be replaced by the electric streetcar. Fortunately, resistance to above-ground wires, corruption in City Hall, and finally the 1906 earthquake, sidetracked those plans. The cable car was kept for the steepest lines, while the streetcar took over the longer, flatter routes.

Informative display at the Cable Car Museum

5 Conductor

The cable car conductor collects fares, but also makes sure that everyone travels safely, and that the grip person has room to work.

6 Turntables

Part of the fun of the cable car experience is being there to watch when the grip person and conductor turn their car around for the return trip. The best view is at Powell and Market Streets.

Cable car traveling along Hyde Street

7 Riding Styles

There is a choice of sitting inside a glassed-in compartment, or outside on wooden benches, or hanging on tightly to poles and standing on the running board. The third option is the best for enjoying the sights, sounds, and smells of San Francisco.

8 Cables

The underground cables are 1.25 inches (3 cm) in diameter and consist of six steel strands of 19 wires, wrapped around a shock-absorbing rope.

9 Routes

The three existing routes cover the Financial District, Nob Hill, Chinatown, North Beach, Russian Hill, and Fisherman's Wharf areas. As these are always important destinations for visitors – and for many residents, too –

most people will find that a cable car ride is a practical, as well as a fun, way to get around.

10 Cable Car Museum

📍 M3 🏛 1201 Mason St at Washington
🕐 10am–4pm Tue–Thu, 10am–5pm Fri–Sun
🌐 cablecarmuseum.org

This site is a museum and the hub of today's cable-car system. The ground floor houses the engines and wheels that wind the cables through the channels and pulleys. Upstairs there are displays of some of the earliest cable cars.

TRANSPORT
The $8 fare is for one cable car ride with no transfers. Consider getting a CityPass, Clipper Card, or a Muni Passport (p141) for multiple journeys.

FISHERMAN'S WHARF

📍 J1–4

Restaurants, shopping, and entertainment are the focus of this vibrant district, attracting locals and visitors alike. Watch fishers at work on Fish Alley unloading their catch, then try the celebrated Dungeness crab, served from November to June, at one of the many seafood restaurants or outdoor crab stands. Nearby, a World War II-era submarine and a Liberty ship recall the city's long history as a port.

2 Ghirardelli Square

The Ghirardelli family used this square *(p83)* as the headquarters of the Ghirardelli Chocolate Company from 1895 until 1962. The site is now home to many shops and restaurants.

eyes. Video presentations and marine specialist guides help you to understand what you're seeing.

4 Boudin Bakery

This is the home of the famous chain of San

1 PIER 39

One of the city's most popular attractions is set on a landscaped pier with Bay views, restaurants, live entertainment, and shops. Families love the bungee jump, mirror maze, and carousel. And San Francisco's beloved and playful sea lion colony at the Pier is a city must-see.

3 Aquarium of the Bay

📍 J4 🌐 aquariumofthe bay.org 🔗

The transparent tunnel of the aquarium visually immerses you in the San Francisco Bay marine habitat, where thousands of different species of ocean fauna disport themselves before your

Freshly baked breads at Boudin Bakery

PIER 39 full of visitors shopping and snacking

working antique and coin-operated arcade games and mechanical musical instruments.

7 The Cannery
Built as a warehouse in 1907, this building underwent a makeover in 1967, and it's now the site of some appealing boutiques, as well as tourist shops.

8 Fish Alley
Pier 47 on Al Scoma Way, nicknamed Fish Alley, is the perfect spot to watch fishing boats return, and see the day's catch being unloaded and prepared for market.

9 Maritime National Historic Park Museum
🅟 J1 🆆 maritime.org ♿
Set inside the former Aquatic Park Bathhouse, this museum features model ships as well as restored maritime murals. It offers great rooftop views of the Aquatic Park Cove.

10 SS Jeremiah O'Brien Liberty Ship
🅟 J3 🆆 ssjeremiah obrien.org ♿🅿
At PIER 39, near North Point Street, floats one of the last two remaining World War II Liberty ships (p71). Take a tour to hear tales of the thousands of troops ferried across the seas in these vessels.

THE PORT OF SAN FRANCISCO

Born out of the California Gold Rush of 1849, the Port of San Francisco stretches nearly 8 miles (13 km) from the Hyde Street Pier to India Basin. It is home to 80 cruise ships, while freighters lumber under the Golden Gate Bridge and ferries, water taxis, fishing boats, and yachts bustle to and from the Ferry Building, Fisherman's Wharf, and Embarcadero piers and marinas.

> 🍴 **EAT**
> To sample some of the best seafood in the city, head straight to the culinary stalwart Scoma's (p107).

Francisco sourdough breadmakers. Try the crusty sourdough bread bowl with New England clam chowder.

5 Anchorage Square Shopping Center
🅟 J3 🅰 2800 Leavenworth St 🆆 anchoragesquare.com
Set in the heart of Fisherman's Wharf, this center has plenty of stores, restaurants, and entertainment.

6 Musée Mécanique
🅟 J3 🅰 Pier 45 at Taylor St 🆆 museemecanique.com
This is one of the world's largest privately owned collections of

SS *Jeremiah O'Brien* docked at Pier 35

4

ALCATRAZ ISLAND

📍 K5 🌐 nps.gov/alcatraz 🅿️🔲

Visible from the crowded shores of Downtown San Francisco, this compelling rocky island and abandoned prison is the city's most notorious attraction. The maximum-security prison on Alcatraz, dubbed "The Rock" by the US Army, was one of the country's busiest detention centers before its closure in 1963. Today, the island is part of the National Park Service, and tours here attract thousands of visitors.

1 Tours

The island can only be accessed by booking a tour (tickets go on sale 90 days in advance). A visit to the prison is brought to life by an excellent audio guide, while rangers lead tours of the island focusing on the Occupation of Alcatraz *(p31)*, the gardens, birdwatching, and more.

2 Building 64

The theater and orientation center are located in the old barracks building behind the ferry jetty. The building also houses a bookstore, exhibits, and a multimedia show providing a historical overview of Alcatraz.

3 Chapel

In the 1920s, a Mission-style military chapel was built above the guardhouse. It was used as living quarters and a school. During the post-1930s phase, it housed prison staff.

4 Cell Blocks

The cell house contains four freestanding cell blocks. The complex was built by military prisoners in 1911 and was once the largest reinforced concrete building in the world.

5 Recreation Yard

Good behavior qualified prisoners for a turn around the walled-in recreation yard. Here,

> **TOP TIP**
>
> It can get cold, and the trails are rough, so wear warm clothes and comfortable shoes.

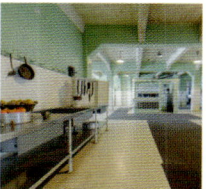

Clockwise from below
Exterior of Building 64, now a museum; corridor separating C and B blocks, nicknamed Broadway; prison kitchen; remains of the warden's house

The former prison on Alcatraz Island

> **EAT**
> Picnicking is allowed at the tables by the dock, but make sure to pack your own food, drinks, and utensils.

they could walk outside of their cells, where they spent between 16 and 23 hours a day.

6 Mess Hall
Meals were one of the few things prisoners had to look forward to, and they were generally well fed to quell rebellion. Note the sample menu at the entrance to the kitchen.

7 Broadway
The corridor that separates C and B blocks was jokingly nicknamed by prisoners after New York City's glittering thoroughfare, famous for its nightlife. The end intersection was named "Times Square."

8 Warden's House
The warden's once-luxurious house is now a ruin after burning down in 1970. Designed in Mission Revival style, the home had 17 large rooms, and sweeping views of the Golden Gate Bridge.

9 Control Room
Guards controlled the security system from this bunker-like facility. Next to the Control Room was the visiting area, where thick glass meant that conversations had to be held over telephones.

10 Lighthouse
Alcatraz was the site of the first lighthouse built on the West Coast, in 1854. The original was replaced in 1909 to tower above the new cell block.

THE HISTORY OF "THE ROCK"

The name "Alcatraz" derives from the Spanish *alcatraces*, for the seabirds that Spanish explorer Juan Manuel de Ayala observed here when he sailed into the Bay in 1775. In 1850, the island was set aside for the US Army to build a citadel, but defense became less of a priority and, in 1907, it became a military prison. In 1934, the Federal Government opened a maximum-security penitentiary here. Yet Alcatraz was not quite the "Devil's Island" that many think it was – the conditions were better than many other prisons.

Stories from The Rock

1. George "Machine Gun" Kelly
Jailed in 1933 for kidnapping, Kelly was given a life sentence, and was sent to Alcatraz for 17 years of that sentence. He was considered a model prisoner by the officers.

2. Al Capone
In 1934, Capone was among the first "official" shipment of prisoners. The infamous gangster was assigned menial jobs and treated like every other inmate.

3. Morton Sobell
Charged with conspiracy to commit treason by spying for the Soviets, Sobell arrived on Alcatraz in 1952 and spent five years as its most famous political prisoner, being a victim of J. Edgar Hoover's witch hunt for Communist subversives. Once freed, Sobell returned to live in San Francisco for many years.

4. Anglin Brothers
The brothers, John and Clarence, are notable as two of the five known inmates to successfully escape from The Rock.

5. Escape from Alcatraz
This 1979 film, starring Clint Eastwood as Frank Morris, who escaped along with the Anglin brothers, is mostly Hollywood fiction, but the depiction of prison life is reportedly accurate.

Clint Eastwood in the film
Escape from Alcatraz

Actor Burt Lancaster as Robert Stroud in *Birdman of Alcatraz*

6. Robert "Birdman" Stroud
The most famous inmate was dubbed the "Birdman of Alcatraz," despite the fact that he was not permitted to conduct his avian studies during his 17 years here. Due to his violent nature and many manslaughter convictions, Stroud spent most of those years in solitary.

7. Birdman of Alcatraz
This 1962 movie presented Robert Stroud as a nature-loving ornithologist, bending historical fact to the service of a good story.

8. Alvin "Creepy" Karpis
Karpis robbed his way through the Midwest between 1931 and 1936, and earned himself the title Public Enemy Number One. He was imprisoned on Alcatraz from 1936 to 1962. He committed suicide in 1979.

9. Frank Wathernam
The last prisoner to leave Alcatraz, on March 21, 1963.

10. The Rock
Hollywood has never lost its fascination with Alcatraz, as can be seen in this 1996 action thriller, starring Sean Connery.

THE OCCUPATION OF ALCATRAZ

In 1969, Richard Oakes and 90 members of the Indians of All Tribes activist group landed on Alcatraz, set up camp, and demanded that the government sell them the island for $24 worth of beads and red cloth. They argued that they were entitled to ownership of the island as reparations after a similar-sized island was taken from the community 300 years earlier. The government considered forcibly removing the occupiers, but growing public support for the Indigenous people forced officials to renew negotiations. However, in January 1970, while playing on the rooftop of one of the buildings, Oakes' youngest daughter slipped and fell to her death; distraught, he and his family decided to abandon their claim. A group of 60 Indigenous people remained, but as the stalemate dragged on, the majority slowly began to leave – only 15 chose to stay. In June 1970, fires ravaged the warden's house, the recreation hall, the officers' club, and the lighthouse. Following this devastation, government troops staged a pre-dawn raid. The remaining Indigenous people were arrested and the 19-month occupation came to an end.

Indigenous people protesting in an attempt to claim the land after the prison closed in 1963

5

CHINATOWN

M4–5, N4–5

Between Stockton Street and Grant Avenue is San Francisco's famous Chinatown, known to be the oldest in the US. This vibrant neighborhood, strung with red lanterns and adorned with dragon lampposts, is full of restaurants, Asian markets, Chinese-inspired architecture, and stores selling everything from kites to cutlery.

1 Dragon Gate
Designed by three Chinese Americans, this triple-pagoda southern entrance to Chinatown was completed in 1970.

2 St. Mary's Square
This square is graced by commemorative

sculptures and plaques, including one of Sun Yat-sen, the father of modern China. There are also memorials honoring Chinese American veterans of World War I and World War II.

3 Golden Gate Fortune Cookie Company
M4 56 Ross Alley goldengate fortunecookies.com
Fortune cookies were invented here. Stop by to watch the workers fold the cookies by hand and to sample flavors like green tea and strawberry.

4 Chinese Six Companies
N4 843 Stochton St
Formally established in 1882, the Chinese Six Companies, also known as the Chinese Consolidated Benevolent Association, promotes mutual aid and business support within the community. The building's brilliant facade is one of the most ornate in Chinatown.

5 Chinatown-Rose Park Muni Station
Opened in 2023, this underground subway stop is part of the Central

> **TOP TIP**
>
> All three cable car lines in San Francisco pass through Chinatown.

Subway system connecting downtown to Chinatown. Throughout the Muni station are permanent art installations by local artists.

6 Chinese Historical Society of America
📍 N5 🏠 965 Clay St
🌐 chsa.org

Designed by architect Julia Morgan in 1932, this building has a learning center and a museum. It features a 15,000-piece collection that documents the Chinese American experience, including an exhibit on Bruce Lee.

7 Stockton Street Chinese Markets

At these popular markets, shops selling Asian produce and other items line the sidewalks. Expect to be elbow-to-elbow with the locals as you navigate through the crowds.

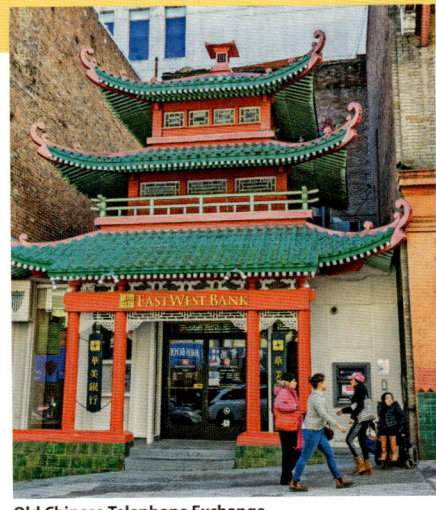

Old Chinese Telephone Exchange

8 Old Chinese Telephone Exchange
📍 M4 🏠 743 Washington St

This three-tiered pagoda is now the East West Bank, and is the most distinctive work of architectural chinoiserie in Chinatown. It served as the telephone exchange up until the 1950s.

9 Chinese Culture Center
📍 M5 🏠 Hilton Hotel, 750 Kearny St, 3rd floor 🌐 cccsf.us

The Chinese Culture Center comprises an art gallery and a small crafts shop, which features the work of Chinese diasporic artists.

10 Temples

There are a number of temples here that incorporate Confucian, Taoist, and Buddhist elements. The Tin How Temple *(p54)*, founded in 1852, is particularly worth visiting.

> 🛍️ **SHOP**
> On Waverly *(on waverly.com)* is an Asian American gift shop with souvenirs by local artists, including stickers, books, and pins.

Distinctive red lanterns strung above Grant Street

Grant Avenue running through San Francisco's Chinatown

GOLDEN GATE PARK

📍 D4 🚪 Entrances on Fulton St, Lincoln Way, Stanyan St & the Great Hwy
🕐 Sunrise–sunset daily 🌐 sfrecpark.org

The city's favorite backyard is a masterpiece of landscape gardening. Here, you'll find the first children's playground in the US, along with the 1914 Herschell-Spillman Carousel. Even on rainy days, there's plenty to do, from exploring the California Academy of Sciences (p38) and the de Young Museum (p40), to visiting the Conservatory of Flowers.

Picturesque setting of the Japanese Tea Garden

1 Japanese Tea Garden

🌐 gggp.org/japanese-tea-garden

This delightful garden is full of bonsai trees, rock gardens, native Japanese plantings, and pagodas.

2 National AIDS Memorial Grove

This memorial was built in remembrance of those who have died from AIDS.

3 Blue Heron Lake

An artificial lake surrounding Strawberry Hill forms an island linked by two stone bridges. Rent a paddleboat to see the Huntington Waterfall, or the Chinese pagoda on the eastern shore.

4 Conservatory of Flowers and Dahlia Dell

The park's oldest building, a copy of one in London's Kew Gardens, is a Victorian-style structure sheltering over 20,000 rare plants. Just southeast is the Dahlia Dell and its hillside terrace.

5 Shakespeare Garden

This English garden features the 200-odd flowers and herbs mentioned in the Bard's works. Bronze plaques quote the relevant passages.

6 Bison Paddock

Opened in 1984, this paddock provides a grazing area for a small herd of bison.

> 🍴 **EAT**
> At the west end of the park is the historic Beach Chalet (p123), serving lunch and dinner during the week and offering brunch on weekends.

The Victorian-style Conservatory of Flowers

Queen Wilhelmina Tulip Garden with its windmill

7 Dutch Windmill and Queen Wilhelmina Tulip Garden

In the northwest corner of the park, the Dutch windmill towers over the tulip garden surrounding it. Both were gifts from the queen of the Netherlands in 1902.

8 Koret Playground

w sfrecpark.org

This is the oldest public playground in the US. It features the Herschell-Spillmann merry-go-round housed in a Greek-inspired structure.

9 Giant Tree Fern Dell and John McLaren Rhododendron Dell

The Giant Tree Fern Dell features a forest of exotic ferns surrounding a small lagoon, while the nearby Rhododendron Dell contains the largest variety (850) of these blooms in any US garden.

10 Music Concourse

This beautifully land-scaped area is home to the Golden Gate Park Bandshell, which hosts free events and summer concerts.

A MIRACLE OF LAND RECLAMATION

This is the largest cultivated urban park in the US. There are 27 miles (43 km) of footpaths, winding through lakes, gardens, waterfalls, and forests, but it was not always so. Before the 1870s, the entire area was untouched scrubland and sandbanks. William Hammond Hall made great progress over two decades, then hired Scottish gardener John McLaren in 1890. "Uncle John," as he was known, made the park his life's work, devoting himself to its perfection until his death in 1943, aged 97.

CALIFORNIA ACADEMY OF SCIENCES

📍 D4 🏛 55 Music Concourse Dr 🕐 9:30am–5pm Mon–Sat, 11am–5pm Sun
🌐 calacademy.org ↗

The California Academy of Sciences lets curious minds get close to nature with exciting exhibits at the Steinhart Aquarium, Morrison Planetarium, and the Kimball Natural History Museum. The building blends in with the natural surroundings of Golden Gate Park, in an environmentally friendly structure with a beautiful roof of local plantlife.

1 Living Roof

The museum is topped with a 108,900-sq-ft (10,100-sq-m) living roof, which is planted with over 1.7 million native Californian plants. Take an elevator up to the rooftop deck to enjoy the views and learn about the benefits of sustainable architecture.

2 California: State of Nature

Developed with the help of Indigenous advisors, this permanent exhibit highlights California's landscapes, biodiversity, and its vastly different state-wide ecosystems through preserved specimens and immersive experiences.

3 Penguin Feeding Time

Part of a "Species Survival Plan," the

TOP TIP

On Thursday nights, those 21 or over can explore and party at the weekly Night-Life series.

African penguins in the Steinhart Aquarium

Indoor Osher Rainforest exhibit

TRANSPORT
Muni buses 5, 7, 44, and the N-Judah metro arrive here. A $3 admission discount applies for visitors who travel via public transit.

penguin colony in the African Hall swims in a 25,000-gallon (95,000-litre) tank. Visitors can watch feedings daily at 10:30am and 3pm.

4 Morrison Planetarium

Fly through space and time to the very limits of the known universe, and gain a new perspective on the planet we call home, with high-tech exhibits and technology, including an all-digital dome. Shows are presented daily.

5 Osher Rainforest

Explore four rainforest habitats in a large multistory glass dome: the Amazonian Flooded Forest, Borneo Forest Floor, Madagascar Rainforest Understory, and the Costa Rica Rainforest Canopy. The conditions of the rainforests are simulated within the dome, creating a suitable home for the 1,600 tropical flora and fauna species, including blue morpho butterflies and spotted Panamanian golden frogs.

6 Discovery Tidepool

Stroke a sea star or pick up a sea slug in this hands-on attraction, which is part of the California Coast exhibits. You don't have to worry about slippery rocks to get close to these coastal creatures. The pool is staffed by volunteers who inform you about the animals and keep them safe.

7 African Hall

Magnificent dioramas display a range of taxidermied African fauna in their natural surroundings, such as the straight-horned oryx, gorillas, antelope, and cheetahs. The human evolution exhibit tracks the fascinating history of our species with fossils of our early ancestors. A lively colony of African penguins, which can be viewed through a vast window, ends the exhibit.

8 Water Planet

Dozens of tanks and a range of interactive media are used to inform all ages of what it takes to survive underwater. A variety of fish, including jellyfish and paddlefish, reptiles, amphibians, and insects are on display.

9 Philippine Coral Reef

This is one of the deepest living coral reef displays in the world. It exhibits a

Bubble corals from the Philippines

range of aquatic life from the reefs and mangroves of the Philippines. Sharks, rays, coral, reef fish, and colorful clams can all be seen here.

10 The Swamp

Part of the Steinhart Aquarium, which holds about 38,000 animals, the Swamp is home to alligator snapping turtles, Claude (the famous alligator with albinism) and frog, rattlesnake, and salamander exhibits.

REDESIGN OF THE DECADE

In 2008, Architect Renzo Piano redesigned the California Academy of Sciences using sustainable materials, to minimize its energy use. At the time, this was the world's first building to be certified Double Platinum by the US Green Building Council.

DE YOUNG MUSEUM

📍 C4 🏛 50 Hagiwara Tea Garden Dr 🕐 9:30am–5:15pm Tue–Sun 🌐 deyoung.famsf.org ♿📷

This immense copper-clad museum looms as a cultural and architectural landmark above a canopy of plane trees in Golden Gate Park. It is a bastion of American, Oceanian, and African art and is home to one of the most impressive textile collections in the US. The de Young also puts on blockbuster temporary exhibitions.

1 Hamon Observation Tower

Ascend the 144-ft (43.8-m) tower to the 360-degree glass-walled observation deck for treetop views of the Music Concourse, the park, the city, and beyond to the Golden Gate Bridge and the Marin Headlands. It closes an hour before the museum.

2 Textiles and Costumes

Three centuries of fiber art and fashion include bark cloth, Central Asian and North Indian silks, the most important Anatolian kilims outside Turkey, European tapestries, and early 20th-century couture.

3 Photography

Spanning the history of the medium, the de Young is strong on 19th-century American and European images, from documentation of the 1894 California Midwinter International Exposition and daguerreotypes to early and contemporary San Franciscan scenes.

4 20th-Century American and Bay Area Artists

Georgia O'Keeffe's *Petunias* is among the contemporary masterworks on display, along with those of local icons – Chiura Obata, Wayne Thiebaud, and Ruth Asawa. It also features a major artwork collection by Black artists of the American South.

5 Art of the Americas

This exhibition features Indigenous artifacts and art spanning 1,000 years, including exquisite 6th-century Teotihuacan mural fragments, Diné

> **TOP TIP**
>
> There's free admission to the Legion of Honor museum *(p123)* with a de Young ticket.

Clockwise from right
The Hamon Observation Tower; a sphinx in the museum garden; a collection of African sculptures; *Boatmen on the Missouri* **by Bingham in the American collection**

(Navajo) weavings, and works by contemporary Inuit artists.

6 Africa and the Pacific

Micronesian and Maori carvings, basketry, and over 1,400 pieces from across the regions are on view, along with Scheller's collection of Masterworks of African Figurative Sculpture, depicting 140 ethnic groups.

7 American Collection

Founded by donations from the Rockefellers, this comprehensive collection, from 1670 to the present, has more than 3,000 decorative arts objects, 800 sculptures, and 1,000 paintings, including *Boatmen on*

Stunning tapestries on display at the museum

the Missouri by George Caleb Bingham.

8 Temporary Exhibits

Wildly popular and requiring advance tickets, some blockbuster exhibitions have included Tutankhamun's treasures and retrospectives on artists Ed Ruscha and Frank Stella.

9 Museum Gardens

Explore the remnants of the California Midwinter International Exposition of 1894 in the surrounding shady walking trails: the Pool of Enchantment, the vases, and the sphinxes.

10 Artful Kids

The de Young welcomes kids to free Saturday art classes, summer camps, and a monthly artist-in-

residence workshop for the whole family. Guided tours for families are followed by studio workshops taught by professional artists.

SAN FRANCISCO MUSEUM OF MODERN ART (SFMOMA)

📍 Q5 🏛 151 3rd St 🕐 10am–5pm Fri–Tue, noon–8pm Thu 🌐 sfmoma.org 🔗📱

Standing proudly next to the Yerba Buena Gardens (p44) art complex, SFMOMA cements San Francisco's reputation as a leading center of modern art. Created in 1935, it moved into its current quarters in 1995, and in May 2016 reopened after a major three-year expansion that tripled its gallery space. The museum offers a dynamic schedule of special exhibitions and permanent collection presentations.

1 Exterior
The facade of the Snøhetta expansion comprises more than 700 uniquely shaped panels which appear to shift in appearance with the changing light.

2 Outdoor Terraces
Six outdoor terraces provide spaces for sculpture installations and highlight dramatic cityscape views.

3 20th-Century American Artists
US artists included here are O'Keeffe, de Kooning, Pollock, Warhol, and Kline. One of the perennial hits is an iconic ceramic

Key
- First floor
- Second floor
- Third floor
- Fourth floor
- Fifth floor
- Sixth floor
- Seventh floor

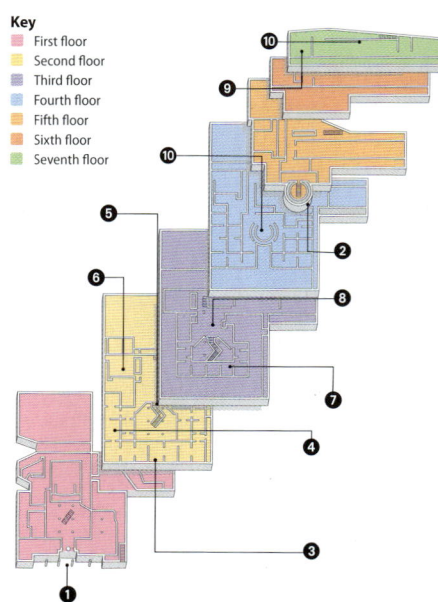

San Francisco Museum of Modern Art Floorplan

EAT
The family-friendly Cafe 5 is in the sculpture garden at SFMOMA. For fine dining, head to In Situ, on the first floor. Sightglass, on the third floor, serves coffee and pastries.

sculpture named *Michael Jackson and Bubbles* by Jeff Koons (1988).

4 20th-Century European Artists
Works by 20th-century European artists are

located on the second floor. Here you will find works by Matisse, Miró, Klee, Picasso, and Magritte, among others.

5 Bay Area Artists
San Francisco Bay Area artists with global

Rippled facade of the SFMOMA

reputations who have pieces on display at SFMOMA include Clyfford Still, Richard Diebenkorn, and Wayne Thiebaud. Bay Area figurative painters in the collection include Elmer Bischoff and David Park. Most noteworthy, perhaps, is *California Artist* (1982), a sculptural self-portrait by Robert Arneson in glazed stoneware.

6 The Living Wall
This incredible living wall provides a unique background for sculpture. Populated with 19,000 plants, including 21 native species, it is an ever-changing work of natural art.

7 Photography
A highlight of the museum, the 15,000-sq-ft (1,394-sq-m) Pritzker Center for Photography houses a collection of over 17,800 photographs.

8 Latin American Artists
Latin American art is represented here by the work of muralist Diego Rivera and Frida Kahlo. Other Latin American representation includes architect Tatiana Bilbao's model *(Not) Another Tower*.

9 Media Arts
Established in 1988, this impressive collection includes multimedia works, moving-image pieces, and video installations by such artists as Brian Eno, Dara Birnbaum, Bill Viola, and Nam June Paik.

10 Special Exhibitions
The museum's special exhibition spaces may feature retrospective exhibitions of the work of modern and contemporary artists, such as multimedia artist Yayoi Kusama, wire sculptor Ruth Asawa, and artist Robert Rauschenberg.

(Not) Another Tower by Tatiana Bilbao

Yerba Buena Gardens

Modern exterior of the Museum of the African Diaspora (MoAD)

1. Museum of the African Diaspora (MoAD)
🅿 Q5 📍 685 Mission St 🕐 11am–6pm Wed–Sat, noon–5pm Sun 🌐 moadsf.org ⮞

The MoAD focuses on contemporary works by Black artists on themes related to the global African diaspora; it reopens after renovation in October 2025 though still hosts events off-site.

2. Yerba Buena Center for the Arts
🅿 Q5 📍 701 Mission St 🕐 11am–5pm Wed–Sun 🌐 ybca.org ⮞

The Center has a gallery of changing exhibitions as well as a theater with a range of performances year-round.

3. Ice Arena and Bowling Center
🅿 Q5 🕐 Hours vary, chech website 📍 750 Folsom St 🌐 shatebowl.com

Enjoy a public skating session or bowl a few frames in the Gardens.

4. Children's Creativity Museum
🅿 Q5 📍 221 4th St 🕐 10am–4pm Fri–Sun 🌐 creativity.org ⮞

This interactive technology and art museum aims to inspire children's creative impulses.

5. Martin Luther King Jr. Memorial
Featuring words of peace in several languages, this multifaceted monument incorporates sculpture, a waterfall, and quotations from the speeches and writings of the civil rights leader.

6. American Bookbinders Museum
🅿 Q4 📍 355 Clementina 🕐 10am–4pm Tue–Sat 🌐 bookbinders museum.org ⮞

This is the only museum in North America dedicated to the art, history, and preservation of bookbinding. Here, you can learn about the craft of hand-binding books.

7. Moscone Center
This building *(p116)* began the renovation of the South of Market (SoMa) district. Most of it is underground; above ground the impression is of glass, girders, and gardens.

8. Rooftop Children's Center and Carousel
🅿 Q5 📍 750 Folsom St

The carousel in this complex dates from 1906. There's also an ice-skating rink, a bowling alley, a learning garden, and an amphitheater.

9. Metreon
🅿 Q4 📍 101 4th St

The city's only IMAX theater is located here, along with popular retailer Target. There's also a food court offering a mix of local vendors, such as the award-nominated Dabao Singapore, and national chains like Chipotle.

10. Yerba Buena Gardens Festival
🌐 ybgfestival.org

A series of free concerts and cultural events takes place over several months at various outdoor venues in Yerba Buena Gardens. Notable performances include the local, family-run Circus Bella, and the London-based jazz-Afrobeat octet, KOKOROKO.

THE SOMA PILIPINAS – FILIPINO CULTURAL HERITAGE DISTRICT

The SOMA Pilipinas – Filipino Cultural Heritage District, covering 1.5 sq miles (4 sq km) of the South of Market neighborhood (SoMa), was designated in 2016. With its headquarters next to the Yerba Buena Gardens, this district was established to honor and celebrate the centuries-long impact of the Filipino community in San Francisco. Today, the work of the SOMA Pilipinas Cultural Heritage District can be seen in the stunning heritage murals lining the streets, the Sentro Filipino Cultural Center, various art galleries and theaters, and annual events, such as the Undiscovered SF Filipinx Block Party in October and the Yum Yams Ube food festival in September. The district offers a diverse schedule of cultural events, performances, and tours that engage with the history of SoMa; for more information, check somapilipinas.org.

A colorful mural in SOMA by artist ChiChai Mateo

WINE COUNTRY

The world-famous Wine Country includes two picturesque valleys, Napa and Sonoma, the hills and dales surrounding them, and over 400 wineries. Napa is more developed for visitors, while Sonoma is a bit more low-key but equally inviting. Napa's downtown area has also become a popular destination for fine dining, tasting rooms, and boutique accommodations.

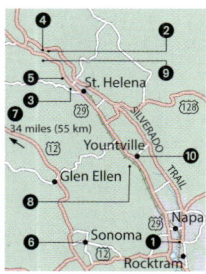

1 Napa Valley Wine Train

W winetrain.com

Leaving from Napa and arriving in St. Helena, or vice versa, you can avoid the traffic and partake of a gourmet meal complemented by local wines. The one-way trip takes three hours and the train features a 1915 Pullman dining car.

2 Sterling Vineyards

W sterlingvineyards.com

An aerial gondola is a unique way to access this hillside winery, and its stunning views are well worth the trip.

3 Beringer Vineyards

W beringer.com

Founded in 1876, this is the oldest Napa Valley winery. Tours, including a self-guided tour, consist of a visit to the 1,000-ft (300-m) wine tunnels, which were carved by hand out of volcanic stone.

4 Clos Pegase

W clospegase.com

Housed in an award-winning Post-Modern structure, this winery offers tours and tastings alongside its collection of modern art. The specialty wines on offer include cabernet, merlot, and portico port.

5 Culinary Institute of America – Greystone and Copia

W ciafoodies.com

This castle-like landmark, built in about 1890,

> ### 🍴 EAT
> For treats like Oprah Winfrey's favorite English muffins, try The Model Bakery *(the modelbakery.com)* in Napa, St. Helena, or Yountville.

houses the West Coast annex of the Culinary Institute of America. Foodies can stock up at the gourmet store, or enjoy cookery and wine classes. The restaurant serves regional cuisine paired with appropriate wines.

Enjoying wine tasting at a winery

6 Sonoma

This town, nestled in the Valley of the Moon, is filled with high-end restaurants, small hotels, and stores. The town also features a State Historic Park with a mission building and structures dating from the early to mid-1800s.

7 Equality Vines

🔲 equalityvines.com

This is the first causewine portfolio vineyard, where proceeds from wine and tasting-tour sales support equality and civil rights-focused causes. The pet-friendly tasting

Hot-air balloons over the vineyards, Yountville

room offers wine-only options or you can choose to pair your wine tasting with a selection of local cheeses, meats, and truffles.

8 Domaine Chandon

🔲 chandon.com

Lovely gardens, a fine restaurant, and sweeping views complement the sparkling wines of this Moët Hennessy showcase.

9 Castello di Amorosa

🔲 castellodiamorosa.com

This re-creation of a Tuscan medieval castle has a moat, watchtowers and a drawbridge, as well as a torture chamber. Take a guided tour and taste the Italian-style wines produced here.

10 Yountville

Hot-air balloons float in the sky over the village of Yountville,

where sweet cottages share the tree-lined streets with restaurants, galleries, upscale hotels, and V Marketplace, a gigantic brick edifice that houses stores, cafés, a spa, and wine-tasting salons.

CALIFORNIA WINE

Since 1857, wine-making has been the mainstay of this area. A phylloxera blight in the early 1900s nearly put an end to it all. In 1976, California wines were put on the global map, when they trounced France in a blind taste-test in Paris. These days, many European producers also have wineries in California.

Wine Country Spas

1. Fairmont Sonoma Mission Inn and Spa
🏠 100 Boyes Blvd, Sonoma
🌐 fairmont.com/sonoma
This famous inn provides an oasis of ultimate indulgence in luxury and refinement. Blessed by natural mineral hot springs, the legendary spa, with inspired architecture and lovely landscaping, exudes understated opulence and serenity.

2. Indian Springs Calistoga
🏠 1712 Lincoln Ave, Calistoga
🌐 indianspringscalistoga.com
Dating from 1862, this hot springs resort with mineral waters from natural geysers has been modernized but has an old-fashioned air about it, with an Olympic-sized heated pool, extensive gardens, and professional spa and mud bath treatments. On-site are lodge rooms and pretty cottages with fireplaces, kitchens, and air-conditioning. There's also a casual restaurant and bar.

3. Health Spa Napa Valley
🏠 1030 Main St, St. Helena
🌐 napavalleyspa.com
In a serene, open-air setting, aches and anxieties are alleviated with a plethora of pampering rituals. For some, that may mean a stimulating fitness workout, or a soothing mud wrap and massage overlooking the tranquil Spa Garden.

4. Calistoga Spa Hot Springs
🏠 1006 Washington St, Calistoga
🌐 calistogaspa.com
Located just off the main street, this spa features four outdoor geothermal mineral pools. Visitors can also try a mud bath, use the gym, or take a yoga or Pilates class. As one of the few family-friendly spas in wine country, it has a wading pool for kids and offers plenty of engaging activities for the whole family. Accommodations include contemporary rooms with kitchenettes.

Entrance to the Roman Spa Hot Springs Resort

5. Roman Spa Hot Springs Resort
🏠 1300 Washington St, Calistoga
🌐 romanspahotsprings.com
Immerse yourself in a volcanic mud bath or indulge in a full-body massage at this Calistoga spa. The pools are naturally heated by the area's geothermal springs, and surrounded by lush garden greenery, creating the feel of a luxurious Roman villa.

6. Mount View Hotel & Spa
🏠 1457 Lincoln Ave, Calistoga
🌐 mountviewhotel.com
A stay in this historic 1917 resort, recipient of California's prestigious Art Deco Preservation Award, offers a range of relaxation and rejuvenation options – from mud, milk, or herbal baths to aromatherapy steam showers, body wraps, massages, or facials – all designed for individuals or couples.

7. Meritage Resort and Spa
🏠 875 Bordeaux Way, Napa
🌐 meritageresort.com
Silence and serenity abide in this luxury resort. The stone-walled,

Old World-style "Estate Cave" contains 12 treatment rooms, with whirlpools and saunas. The four-star hotel rooms are spacious; ask about the special packages on offer. On site, you will find restaurants, a large fitness studio, and a sports bar.

8. Rendez Veuve Spa
📍 6481 Washington St, Yountville
🌐 theestateyountville.com

"Champagne flows as freely as the possibilities" is the motto of the first Veuve Clicquot-inspired spa, which opened in 2024 at The Estate Yountville boutique hotel and vineyard. Aside from the bubbly, guests can indulge in gold-themed treatments, including a golden shimmer scrub, shimmer oil, or a collagen mask. The spa also features Swiss experience showers, a cold plunge bath, and 12 treatment rooms.

9. Silverado Resort and Spa
📍 1600 Atlas Peak Rd, Napa
🌐 silveradoresort.com

This luxury resort in the wine country, covering 2 sq miles (5 sq km), is studded by oak trees and anchored by a historic mansion housing restaurants and lounges. It's also home to two championship golf courses, dozens of swimming pools, and a tennis complex. The upscale spa offers 12 rooms for top-notch body treatments, plus private garden pavilions, a nail and hair salon, a café, yoga classes, and workout facilities.

10. Boon Hotel + Spa
📍 14711 Armstrong Woods Rd, Guerneville 🌐 boonhotels.com

Among the beautiful and towering redwoods of the Russian River area, this small, peaceful, adults-only inn offers an invigorating retreat from modern life. Body treatments include CBD-infused and Swedish massages, and soothing facials with seaweed anti-wrinkle masks. Included in your stay are use of the pool and hot tub, and evening wine tastings on selected weekends. The restaurant serves Russian River wines and sources ingredients from local suppliers or from its garden.

Stately mansion of the Silverado Resort and Spa

TOP 10 OF EVERYTHING

Victorian houses off North Beach

HISTORIC SITES

1 Mission Dolores
This 18th-century Spanish mission (*p115*) is the oldest building in the city. Its 4-ft (1.2-m) thick adobe walls and red-tile roofs are typical of the "Mission Style" seen all over California.

2 Jackson Square
This neighborhood (*p96*) has some of the city's oldest and loveliest buildings, including the iconic Transamerica Pyramid nearby. It is also one of the few places spared in the 1906 earthquake.

3 War Memorial Opera House
Inaugurated in 1932, this building (*p97*) is dedicated to World War I soldiers. In 1945 it hosted the plenary sessions that preceded the founding of the UN and, in 1951, it was the site of the signing of the peace treaty between the US and Japan.

4 The Presidio
More than 350 buildings, which spent 200 years in a military enclave, have been repurposed as museums, restaurants, and recreational facilities (*p104*). Highlights include the Presidio Tunnel Tops park, Civil War barracks, Victorian mansions, a World War II memorial, the Walt Disney Family Museum, and the heritage gallery in the Officers' Club.

5 North Beach
This entire area (*p95*) resonates with the history of the early Italian residents, as well as with the iconoclastic legacy of the Beat generation, who brought the neighborhood worldwide fame. Historic churches and the City Lights Bookstore (*p98*) stand as clear landmarks, while equally historic saloons and cafés are worth seeking out.

6 Ferry Building
🚋 H2 📍 Embarcadero at Market
Once the tallest building in the city, with a 235-ft- (71.6-m-) high clock tower modeled after the Giralda tower in Seville in 1898, this was once the headquarters of streetcars and ferryboats. Fireboat crews saved the tower from the 1906 fire.

The Ferry Building with its iconic clock tower

Fountain in Huntington Park at Nob Hill

7 Nob Hill

Home to historic hotels and remnants of the age of prosperity of the railroad barons *(p96)*. The Fairmont Hotel (1907) is famous for the Tonga Room & Hurricane Bar, and the Mark Hopkins (1939) is crowned by the Top of the Mark lounge. Grace Cathedral's spires tower over everything.

8 Haight-Ashbury

This was the epicenter *(p111)* of the hippie movement that gave birth to the famous "Summer of Love" in 1967. An aura of this past can still be found in its cafés, vintage clothing shops, and the house at 710 Ashbury Street where band members of the Grateful Dead lived from 1965–68.

9 The Fillmore

This venue (livenation.com/venue/the-fillmore-events) was one of the legendary homes of psychedelic rock in the 1960s. Along with the Avalon Ballroom and the Winterland (both now gone), this is where the San Francisco sound found its first audience.

10 Fort Point National Historic Site

🅟 C1 🅐 Marine Drive

At this much-photographed site under the Golden Gate Bridge, swords, guns, and cannons are on view at a fortification that was built during the Civil War to protect the city from an attack by sea, which never came. Rangers and costumed docents give free tours of the gunpowder store-house, the barracks, and the museum.

TOP 10 HISTORIC FIGURES

1. John Muir
A keen promoter of the National Parks movement. The Muir Woods *(p91)* are named in his honor.

2. John C. Fremont
Instrumental in the US annexation of California in the mid-1800s, Fremont dubbed the Bay strait the "Golden Gate."

3. Ansel Adams
Born in 1902, Adams was a well-known photographer and environmentalist. His work later became important for local conservation efforts.

4. Carlos Santana
A mural in the Mission District honors Santana, who moved to San Francisco from Mexico as a child and later became an iconic figure in the city's music scene. He pioneered a fusion of rock and roll, blues, Latin American jazz, and Afro-Cuban rhythms, and has won many Grammy Awards.

5. Dr. Dian Fossey
One of the world's foremost experts on primatology, Dr. Fossey helped pave the way for women in zoo-logical studies.

6. Isadora Duncan
This pioneer of modern dance lived a life of creativity and adventure.

7. Dorothea Lange
An acclaimed photojournalist known for documenting the plight of common folks during the 1930s Great Depression.

8. Harvey Milk
The first openly gay politician to become a member of the Board of Supervisors was assassinated in 1978.

9. Dianne Feinstein
One of the movers and shakers of San Francisco politics in recent decades, she was a US senator from 1992 until 2023.

10. Willie Brown
The first Black mayor of San Francisco, Brown is a longtime influence in San Francisco's political scene.

ARCHITECTURAL HIGHLIGHTS

1 Palace of Fine Arts
E1 · 3301 Lyon St · palaceoffinearts.org
This Neo-Classical building, today used for shows, was designed by Bernard Maybeck for the Pan-Pacific Exposition of 1915 and was inspired by the engravings of Giovanni Piranesi.

2 Grace Cathedral
The third largest Episcopal church (*p95*) in the US was executed in the medieval French Gothic style. Its stained-glass windows glow atop Nob Hill.

3 Civic Center
This complex (*p97*) is centered on City Hall, a Baroque Revival paragon (1915) with a golden dome, attracting tourists and wedding parties for photos on its curving marble staircase decorated with filigree iron and gilt. The other buildings are in the Beaux Arts style. Befitting the city that started the Gold Rush, gilt is everywhere.

4 555 California Street
N5 · 555 California St
This 52-story structure, known previously as the Bank of America Center, was the first skyscraper in the city, erected in 1972. The color was a mistake – the granite that faces it was supposed to be pink, not brown, but by the time the delivery was made, it was too late to change it.

5 Coit Tower
This Art Deco landmark (*p98*) is named for the benefactor Lillie Coit, who left a substantial bequest to beautify her beloved city. The observation deck offers great views. Depression-era murals (*p84*) decorate the lobby.

6 Cathedral of St. Mary of the Assumption
Some critics dismiss this parabolic form (*p55*), but the soaring curves draw attention upward, in the same way that tracery and vaulting do in Gothic cathedrals.

7 San Francisco Museum of Modern Art
This striking post-modern oculus (*p42*) was designed by architect Mario Botta. It was augmented by the Norwegian firm, Snøhetta, with a rippling facade replicating the waters and fog of the bay.

8 Alamo Square
E4
With a downtown backdrop and a sweeping greensward below, these vividly hued late 1800s Victorian mansions (or "Painted Ladies") are on the 700 block of Steiner Street.

Neo-Classical Palace
of Fine Arts

9 Haas-Lilienthal House
M1 ⬛ 2007 Franklin St
⬛ haas-lilienthalhouse.org ⬛⬛

This Queen Anne-style mansion, built in 1886, is one of the few Victorian beauties in the city that accepts visitors. It offers a wonderful glimpse into the way of life among San Francisco's upper-middle classes from about 1890 to 1920. Gables, a turret, and fancy embellishments make this a showstopper on Franklin Street. The house is only open for guided tours, on select Saturdays at noon, 1pm, and 2pm.

10 Transamerica Pyramid
N5 ⬛ 600 Montgomery St
⬛ transamericapyramid.com

A sparkling white obelisk made out of crushed quartz, the pyramid is one of the most iconic symbols of San Francisco. At 853 ft (260 m), it is the second-tallest building in San Francisco. At its base is Redwood Park, with 50 towering Santa Cruz redwood trees. As part of a $400 million redevelopment, its lobby now features several dining establishments, including cafés and fine-dining restaurants.

The Transamerica Pyramid, one of the city's classic sights

TOP 10 RELIGIOUS CENTERS

1. Cathedral of St. Mary of the Assumption
F3 ⬛ 1111 Gough St
This church is a unique and contemplative space, notable for its 18-story, brutalist design.

2. Grace Cathedral
The Grace Cathedral (p95) mixes Italian Renaissance with Gothic architecture in a wholly American blend.

3. Temple Emanu-El
D3 ⬛ 2 Lake St
Inspired by Istanbul's Hagia Sophia, this 1926 synagogue has the city's longest-serving congregation.

4. Mission Dolores
This Spanish mission (p115) was built in the 18th century by the Native Ohlone.

5. Zen Center
F4 ⬛ 300 Page St
The Center offers daily meditations, monastic retreats and workshops.

6. Glide Memorial United Methodist Church
Q3 ⬛ 330 Ellis St
A community-focused church, Glide Memorial seeks to make a positive impact throughout the city. It hosts exuberant celebrations on Sundays.

7. Saints Peter and Paul Church
This North Beach "Italian Cathedral" (p98) has a sculpture of da Vinci's *The Last Supper*.

8. Tin How Temple
G2 ⬛ 125 Waverly Pl
Mazu, the Taoist goddess of the sea, is honored in this Chinatown temple.

9. St. John Coltrane Church
E3 ⬛ 2097 Turk St
The famous jazz musician St. John Coltrane is canonized by this congregation. Services consist of a sermon and worship music.

10. First Unitarian Universalist Church
P1 ⬛ 1187 Franklin St
Since 1850, this progressive church has always welcomed people of all faiths and creeds.

MUSEUMS

1 de Young Museum

This bastion (p40) of American, Oceanian, and African art is a landmark in Golden Gate Park, topped by a 144-ft (44-m) observation tower. Founded with pieces from the 1894 California Midwinter Fair, the Oceanic and African groupings have been expanded with private collections. There is a sculpture garden and a collection of American art from colonial times to the 20th century.

2 Oakland Museum of California (OMCA)

1000 Oak St, Oakland 11am–5pm Wed–Sun museumca.org

California's only museum exclusively dedicated to documenting the state's art, history, and natural sciences, the OMCA has over two million objects in its collection. The museum chronicles the California and Bay Area history, featuring interdisciplinary exhibitions on topics like the Black Power movements in California and the historical mapping of the state. There's also a kids' play space that re-creates California's natural environments.

3 California Academy of Sciences

The environmentally friendly architecture of the Academy's building (p38) emphasizes ecological and sustainable features and blends in with the natural surroundings of the park. The museum covers virtually every aspect of the natural world.

4 San Francisco Museum of Modern Art (SFMOMA)

The SFMOMA (p42) has seven floors of 20th- and 21st-century art, free public areas, outdoor terraces, a café, a restaurant, and a gift shop.

5 Asian Art Museum

R2 200 Larkin St 1–8pm Thu, 10am–5pm Fri–Mon asianart.org

Set in the old Main Library, which was restructured by architect Gae Aulenti, this museum is home to a vast collection of Chinese, Korean, Japanese, Himalayan, and Southeast Asian works. It has the largest outdoor art terrace in the US, and a new pavilion for special exhibitions.

6 Maritime Museum

F1 900 Beach St, Aquatic Park 10am–4pm Wed–Sun nps.gov/safr

Located inside a 1939 bathhouse, this museum is awash with ship models, figureheads, maritime paintings, and seagoing relics including scrimshaw.

Life-size dinosaur model at the California Academy of Sciences

Auguste Rodin's *The Thinker* at the Legion of Honor

7 Legion of Honor

This museum *(p123)* is set in a building commemorating the Californian soldiers who died in World War I. Four thousand years of American and European art are displayed here, as well as antiquities from ancient Egypt, Greece, and Rome.

8 San Francisco Museum of Craft and Design

📍H5 🏛2569 Third St 🕐10am–5pm Wed–Sat, noon–5pm Sun 🔒Major public hols 🌐sfmcd.org ♿

This unique museum celebrates modern craft and design through innovative exhibitions. Many lectures, shows, and programs are organized for children.

9 Museum of the African Diaspora (MoAD)

One of the few museums dedicated to African diasporic art, the MoAD *(p44)* focuses on contemporary and emerging artists. Although the museum is currently closed for renovations, it continues to host events off-site and plans to reopen in October 2025 to celebrate its 20th anniversary.

10 Society of California Pioneers

📍D2 🏛300 Fourth St 🕐Hours vary, chech website 🌐california pioneers.org

On display here is a collection of historical exhibits from 19th- and 20th-century California. The gallery features annually rotating exhibits from the private collection.

TOP 10 LESSER-KNOWN MUSEUMS

1. Cable Car Museum
Located inside a cable barn, this free museum *(p25)* traces the history of the city's iconic transit system.

2. GLBT Historical Society Museum
📍E5 🏛4127 18th St
This museum curates stories of the LGBTQ+ community in the city.

3. SFO Museum
🏛San Francisco International Airport
The country's only accredited museum in an airport houses dozens of exhibits throughout its terminals.

4. The Beat Museum
🏛540 Broadway
This museum is dedicated to the history and legacy of the Beat generation.

5. Pacific Pinball Museum
🏛1510 Webster St, Alameda
Play on 90 pinball machines spanning decades at this interactive museum.

6. The American Bookbinders Museum
📍G3 🏛355 Clementina St
This is North America's only museum dedicated to the history of bookbinding.

7. David Ireland House
📍F5 🏛500 Capp St
Take a guided tour through the workspace and home of the late artist.

8. Walt Disney Family Museum
📍D2 🏛104 Montgomery St, Presidio
This museum tells the history of the man behind the Disney empire.

9. Tenderloin Museum
📍Q3 🏛398 Eddy St
Learn about the rich history of the city's most colorful neighborhood.

10. Wells Fargo History Museum
📍N5 🏛420 Montgomery
Observe relics such as gold nuggets at this free banking museum.

ART GALLERIES

1 SOMArts Cultural Center
G4 934 Brannan St between 8th & 9th sts Noon–7pm Tue–Fri, noon–5pm Sat somarts.org
Group and solo shows, music, and readings all take place here. Founded in 1975, SOMArts is a city-owned cultural center with two exhibition spaces, a 250-seat theater, and printmaking, photography, and design studios.

2 City Art Gallery
Owned and operated by the artists themselves, this cooperative gallery *(p118)* prides itself on making artwork accessible as well as affordable to those interested in collecting or gifting art. Showcasing the work of around 200 local artists – some new, some known and established – the gallery exhibits an array of styles and media through changing exhibitions.

3 Fraenkel Gallery
P4 49 Geary St 10:30am–5:30pm Tue–Fri, 11am–5pm Sat fraenkelgallery.com
Opened in 1979, the gallery held an exhibition early on featuring NASA's lunar photographs, and this set the tone for what was to follow. Soon came exhibitions by Eugene Atget, Edward Weston, Hiroshi Sugimoto, and Diane Arbus, and later, the Bechers, Adam Fuss, and Sol LeWitt. Projects have brought together work across a variety of media.

4 Pacific Heritage Museum
N5 608 Commercial St (415) 399-1124 10am–4pm Tue–Sat
This museum and gallery has occupied the historic US Sub-Treasury building dating to 1875, on top of which the East West Bank has been built. The bank sponsors the museum, which focuses on the art of the Pacific Rim, aiming to bring the work of Asian artists to a wider audience. Exhibitions feature many pieces on loan from private collections.

5 Gallery Wendi Norris
F4 436 Jackson St 11am–6pm Tue–Sat gallerywendi norris.com
This dynamic and extremely stylish contemporary art venue in North Beach hosts exhibitions of celebrated American and international works, including those by prominent artists from China, Japan, South Korea, and Russia. Some Bay Area artists are also featured in the gallery. The staff is on hand to provide advice to amateur and serious collectors alike about the contemporary art market.

6 Museo Italo Americano
F1 Fort Mason Center, Building C Noon–4pm Tue–Sat, 10am–2pm Sun; Mon by appt only museoitaloamericano.org
A museum, gallery, and community center for San Francisco's Italians. Regular changing exhibitions

Interior of the SOMArts
Cultural Center

might focus on the work of either an individual Italian artists more generally, or on aspects of Italian culture.

7 111 Minna Gallery
📍 P5 🏠 111 Minna St 🕐 Hours vary, chech website 🌐 111minnagallery.com

A SoMa district institution since 1993, 111 Minna turns gallery-going into a social event. Visitors can make use of a bar set within the exhibition space. The gallery features notable local and international artists, and also hosts live performance events.

8 Galería de la Raza
📍 G5 🏠 2779 Folsom St 🕐 Noon–5pm Wed–Fri 🌐 galeriadelaraza.org

This gallery has grown to become one of the most respected Latin American arts organizations in the country. It promotes awareness and appreciation of Latin American/Chicano art including painting, photography, and sculpture. Galería de la Raza also provides a platform for the performing arts, spoken word nights, as well as for projecting digital murals on the building's facade.

9 Berggruen Gallery
📍 Q5 🏠 10 Hawthorne St 🕐 10am–5pm Mon–Fri 🌐 berggruen.com

One of the most popular galleries for the exhibition and sale of modern American and European art since the 1970s. Their displays have included artworks from masters such as de Kooning, Calder, and Matisse.

10 San Francisco Arts Commission Gallery
📍 R1 🏠 401 Van Ness Ave 🕐 Noon–5pm Wed–Sat 🌐 sfartscommission.org/gallery

Opened in 1970, this was one of the first galleries dedicated to showing the work of emerging Bay Area artists. In addition, the Gallery Slide Registry contains images by more than 500 professional artists from across the US.

TOP 10
PUBLIC ART SITES

1. Balmy Alley
📍 G6 🏠 24th & 25th sts between Harrison & Treat
The most famous set of murals in town, by local Latin American artists.

2. Moraga Steps
The stairway off 16th Ave features a mosaic pattern covering all 163 steps.

3. Bay Lights
Leo Villareal's light sculpture on the Bay Bridge features 25,000 LED lights.

4. Fort Mason
The Fort Mason Center for Arts and Culture (p105) has rotating exhibits.

5. Women's Building
📍 F5 🏠 18th St between Valencia & Guerrero
The work of seven women painters graces the facade.

6. The Duboce Bikeway Mural
📍 F4 🏠 Duboce St between Church & Market
This mural chronicles a bike ride from Downtown to Ocean Beach.

7. Golden Gate Park
The Music Concourse (p37) is home to many sculptures from world's fairs.

8. Rincon Center
📍 H2 🏠 Mission, Howard, Steuart & Spear sts
These 1948 murals by Russian Anton Refregier trace Californian history.

9. Financial District
See *Transcendence* in front of 555 California Street and the Day for Night lights atop the Salesforce Tower.

10. Beach Chalet
Depression-era murals depicting famous San Franciscans (p123).

Beach Chalet mural

WRITERS AND NOTABLE RESIDENTS

1 Jack Kerouac
Arriving from New York in 1947, it was Kerouac (1922–69) who coined the term "Beat." He and his companions – Neal Cassady, Allen Ginsberg, Lawrence Ferlinghetti, and others – initiated the new politics of dissent and free love that led, within a decade, to the hippie movement. His novel *On the Road* (1957) galvanized a generation.

2 Isabel Allende
One of the world's most widely read Spanish-language authors, this Chilean American Bay Area resident is famous for her magical realism in *The House of the Spirits*, *City of the Beasts*, *Eva Luna*, and *Of Love and Shadows*. She received the Presidential Medal of Freedom in 2014.

3 Robin Williams
A resident of the Bay Area from when he was a teenager, TV and movie star Williams (1951–2014) began his career as a stand-up comedian in San Francisco clubs and was credited with kick-starting the comedy "renaissance" of the 1970s. Beloved by and friendly to locals, he was known for his generosity to Bay Area charities.

4 Jack London
Adventurer and author of frontier tales such as *White Fang*, *The Sea Wolf*, and *The Call of the Wild*, Jack London (1876–1916) grew up in Oakland. A museum of his memorabilia is now housed there, in a recon-struction of the log cabin he lived in while prospecting for gold in the Yukon

Jack London statue in Oakland

New York Yankees baseball player, Joe DiMaggio

territory. His fiction is based on his experiences in the untamed West and the social inequality he saw in boomtown San Francisco.

5 Joe DiMaggio
DiMaggio (1914–99) was born and began his baseball career in San Francisco. His 56-game hitting streak with the New York Yankees made him a legend. He married Marilyn Monroe in San Francisco.

6 William Randolph Hearst
An animated publisher of the *San Francisco Examiner* who built the nation's largest newspaper chain in the late 1800s, Hearst (1863–1951) influenced the American press with his "yellow journalism" tactics, built Hearst Castle, served twice in the US House of Representatives, and inspired the movie *Citizen Kane*.

7 Francis Ford Coppola
The director of *The Godfather* makes San Francisco the home of his American Zoetrope productions, and has also branched out into other enterprises. His Inglenook winery in the Napa Valley is one of the best.

8 Fred Korematsu
A pioneer of civil rights in San Francisco and the Bay Area, Fred Korematsu (1919–2005) defied US government orders to be interred during World War II on the basis of his Japanese heritage. The ruling in his case was later overturned, and he spent the rest of his life fighting for civil rights. He was awarded the Presidential Medal of Freedom in 1998.

9 Armistead Maupin
Maupin's *Tales of the City* were serialized in the *San Francisco Chronicle* before being published in book form. They are lighthearted paeans to the lifestyle of LGBTQ+ San Francisco in the 1970s.

10 Carlos Santana
A Mexican American who grew up in San Francisco and was influenced by Bay Area's 1960s jazz and folk musicians, Santana founded a band that pioneered Afro-Latin-blues-rock fusion at the Fillmore West, in other clubs around the area, and at Woodstock. He went on to top the *Billboard* charts for decades, selling more than 100 million records.

Famous guitarist Carlos Santana at a concert

TOP 10 FIGURES FROM THE 1960S

1. José Sarria (1922–2013)
This influential drag queen became the first openly gay person to run for public office in 1961.

2. Maya Angelou (1928–2014)
Born in San Francisco, this poet published her first autobiography to international acclaim in 1969.

3. Joan Didion (1934–2021)
A native Californian, Didion captured the mood of a generation and the counterculture of the 1960s in her 1968 book *Slouching Towards Bethlehem*.

4. Ken Kesey (1935–2001)
A powerful, revolutionary writer, his Magic Bus and Trips Festival set the tone for the entire hippie movement.

8. Grace Slick (b. 1939)
A quintessentially San Franciscan voice, Slick fronted Jefferson Airplane and wrote several of the band's most famous songs, including "White Rabbit" and "Somebody to Love."

5. Huey Newton (1942–89)
Oakland's founder of the Black Panthers, a group committed to civic and social change.

6. Jerry Garcia (1942–95)
Patriarch of the San Francisco sound, his Grateful Dead band continued to tour until his death in 1995.

7. Mario Savio (1942–96)
The UC Berkeley student launched the Free Speech Movement on the campus in the late 1960s.

9. Janis Joplin (1943–70)
This Texan singer is celebrated for her powerful mezzo-soprano vocals and is known as the queen of the San Francisco sound. She moved into her second-floor apartment at 635 Ashbury Street with her partner, Peggy Caserta, in 1967.

10. Patty Hearst (b. 1954)
The newspaper heiress, kidnapped by the Symbionese Liberation Army in 1974, was apparently converted and took part in an armed robbery.

PARKS AND GARDENS

1 Marina Green
📍 E1

Within sight of the Golden Gate Bridge, and across the street from photogenic 1930s mansions and the Palace of Fine Arts (p54), are several blocks of Bayside greensward, which are perfect for picnicking and people-watching. On weekends, observe kite-flyers, joggers, and cyclists, as well as yoga, tai chi, and Zumba practitioners. Some people work out on the seven-station fitness circuit.

2 Mission Dolores Park
📍 F5

Nestled in a corner of the Mission District and situated high on a hill is this large park. It features several basketball and tennis courts, a soccer field, and a playground. The southern part of the park offers great views across the Bay.

3 Fort Mason
📍 F1

The rolling lawn above Fort Mason Center, known as the Great Meadow, is a relatively little-used park, but it's great for taking a siesta, tossing a frisbee, or just strolling through to take in the spectacular views from the cliffs.

4 Golden Gate Park

One of the largest city parks in the US is also one of the most diverse, and all of it was brought forth from what was once scrub and dunes. The park also features first-rate cultural attractions such as the de Young Museum (p40).

5 Lafayette Park
📍 F2

This is another of the double-blocked hilltop gardens in Pacific Heights – a leafy green haven of pine and euca-lyptus trees. Steep stairways lead to the summit of the park, which has delightful views.

6 Conservatory of Flowers

Shipped around Cape Horn from England and erected in Golden Gate Park in 1879, this magnificent five-story Victorian greenhouse (p36) contains a jungle of trees, palms, aquatic plants, and flowers. There are thousands of orchids, an enchanting butterfly enclosure, and lily ponds. Plant lovers come from around the

Conservatory of Flowers at the Golden Gate Park

world to learn about endangered flora and horticultural innovations like aquascaping.

7 Rincon Park
📍 H2

Situated just south of the Ferry Building Marketplace on the Embarcadero pedestrian promenade, *Cupid's Span*, a 60-ft- (18-m-) tall sculpture of a red-feathered bow and arrow, marks the location of this bayside park. The lawns and benches afford awesome views of the San Francisco–Oakland Bay Bridge, the city's spectacular skyline, and passing ships.

8 Yerba Buena Gardens

In the South of Market museum district, surrounding the Yerba Buena Center for the Arts *(p44)*, are lawns, shade trees, gardens, and water features, which all create a verdant setting for whimsical outdoor sculptures. Don't miss the 50-ft- (15-m-) wide Martin Luther King Jr. waterfall.

9 Sigmund Stern Recreation Grove

Famous for its free summer concerts, Sigmund Stern Recreation Grove *(p84)* is a leafy recreation complex containing playing fields, tennis and croquet courts, as well as a playground and a dog park. Pine Lake is popular for jogging, and there are plenty of good picnic spots under the eucalyptus, redwood, and pine trees.

10 The Presidio

This vast swath of greenery *(p104)* became part of the city's parklands in 1994. It is a beautiful space with wonderful views over the Bay, and is home to many chic restaurants and museums *(p104)*. At its heart is the sprawling Presidio Tunnel Tops national park, which offers stunning views of the Golden Gate Bridge. The park is open daily, attracting both tourists and locals who come to enjoy the wooded areas, walking trails, and picnic spots.

Hiking a trail in the park at the Presidio

Clockwise from above
Footpath in Golden Gate Park's Japanese Garden; the vintage carousel at Koret playground; boaters on Stow Lake

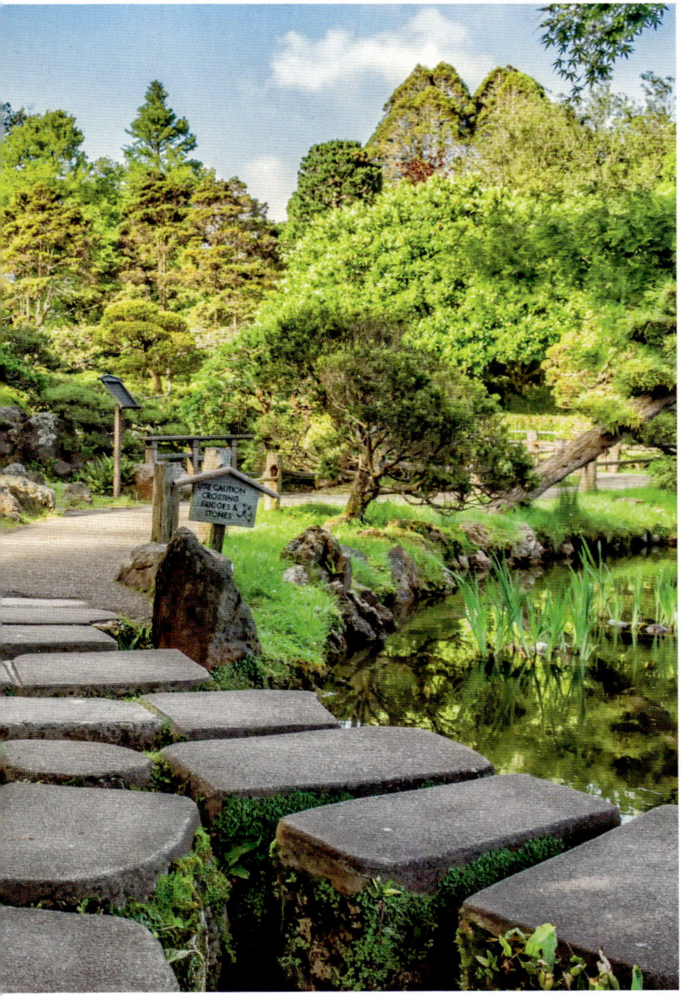
USE CAUTION
CROSSING
BRIDGES &
STONES

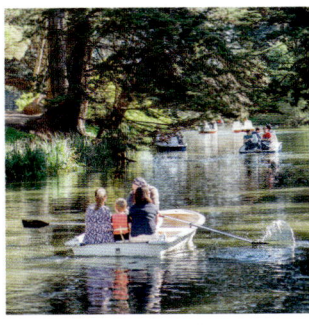

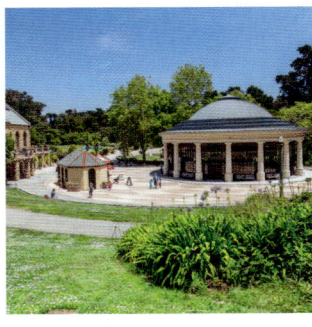

BEACHES

1 Baker Beach
📍 C2

This 1-mile (1.5-km) stretch of sandy beach, with its perfect views of the Golden Gate Bridge, is the most famous in the city. It's great for sunbathing, dog-walking, picnicking, or jogging, but signs warn off swimmers because of riptides.

2 Stinson Beach

Three miles (5 km) of sand *(p132)*, coupled with the fact that Marin County often has fine weather even when the rest of the coast is covered in fog, make this one of the most popular beaches in the Bay Area. It can be busy when it's sunny.

3 Muir and Red Rock Beaches
📍 Muir Beach: off Hwy 1 on Pacific Way; Red Roch: 5.5 miles (9 hm) north of Muir on Pacific Way

These two beaches, just south of Stinson, are the most famous nude beaches north of San Francisco. Both are sandy curves within their own coves, protected from wind and prying eyes by rocky cliffs. The only caveat is that you'll need sturdy walking shoes to get down the rough paths that lead to them from the parking lots.

4 China Beach
📍 B2

This is the poshest beach in San Francisco, being adjacent to the exclusive Sea Cliff neighborhood. Despite its pedigree, California law requires that all coastal areas remain public, although access roads to them can be private. China Beach is small and protected from the wind, there's plenty of parking, and it's a pleasant walk to the sand.

5 Pacifica Beaches
📍 Hwy 1

A 20-minute drive south of the city are several Pacific Ocean beaches popular with surfers, swimmers, and families. A favorite of beginner surfers, Linda Mar Beach has restrooms and showers, and connects by a breezy trail to Rockaway Beach. Sharp Park Beach has picnic sites, a fishing pier with a café, parking, and nature trails.

6 Bolinas Beach

This hidden-away Marin beach *(p132)* tends to be windy and is mostly used by dog-walkers and kayakers. It's sandy, with a backdrop of rocky cliffs. If you walk north, you'll find sheltered nooks, where some sun worshippers bask in the nude, although there is a rarely enforced city ordinance against it.

**Golden Gate Bridge
as seen from Baker Beach**

of seabirds. A clothing-optional beach, Marshall's is popular with open-minded locals and the city's LGBTQ+ residents. Access is via the steep Batteries to Bluffs Trail or from popular North Baker Beach, also a nude beach. Swimming is prohibited due to strong currents.

7 Ocean Beach

Some 4 miles (6.5 km) long and quite broad, this is the city's largest beach by far *(p123)*, but probably the worst for entering the water safely. It starts at Cliff House and continue beyond the city limits, turning into picturesque dunes at its southern end. The beach is popular with locals for its communal fire pits during burn season from March to October.

8 Marshall's Beach
🅿 C1

Also known as Lands End Beach, Marshall's Beach is secluded almost beneath the Golden Gate Bridge, with stunning sea views and good sightings

9 Aquatic Park

Shielded by a fishing pier shaped like a horseshoe, this *(p104)* is a human-made lagoon near Fisherman's Wharf, with a sandy beach, a seawall for lounging, restrooms, and a walkway making it accessible to wheelchairs and bikes. This is the number-one spot from which to watch the Fourth of July fireworks. Swimming is sometimes prohibited due to water quality.

10 Crissy Field East Beach
🅿 D1

On the paved Bay Trail between the yacht harbor in the Marina District and Crissy Field, with dazzling Golden Gate Bridge and Alcatraz views, this is one of the only beaches where swimming is safe from undertows and currents. On site are picnic tables and grills, restrooms, lawns for lounging, and free parking.

OUTDOOR ACTIVITIES

1 Hiking
The Bay Area is replete with excellent hiking trails perfect for getting out and enjoying nature. Lands End has wild terrain to scramble over (p125), and Mount Tamalpais is crisscrossed with trails (p133), but just scaling the city's hills is enough hiking for most people.

2 Swimming
Some hotels and the Embarcadero YMCA (ymcasf.org) have pools, and close-to-shore swimming can be enjoyed at a few spots, including the protected cove at Aquatic Park (p104) and the shallow waters off Crissy Field (p67) – kids wade in the tidal marsh here, too.

3 Skating
It's great fun to watch inline and roller skaters show off their skills. Skatin' Place (saintcloudskatinplace. com) in Golden Gate Park has weekend skate rental from noon to 6pm. Skating can also be enjoyed on the paved path at Marina Green (p62).

4 Biking
Cycling is big in San Francisco. Don't miss biking across the Golden Gate Bridge. Rent bikes from private companies such as Avenue Cyclery (avenuecyclery.com) or the SFMTA-Lyft partnership via Bay Wheels.

5 Running
Running paths line several of the Bay's shores, with great views all around. Since the restoration of Crissy Field, the Golden Gate Promenade (p104) has been an inspiring run – and, of course, Golden Gate Park is full of endless opportunities for jogging. If organized running is your thing, try the Bay to Breakers (bayto breakers.com) or the San Francisco Marathon (thesfmarathon.com).

6 Tennis
There are several public tennis courts in San Francisco. Visit the website of the Recreation and Park department (sfrecpark.org) to reserve a time slot at public tennis, padel, and pickleball courts for free. The Golden Gate Park (rec.us/sfrecpark) courts charge a small fee; make sure you book in advance. Most public outdoor courts are open from sunrise to sunset. Indoor courts are the purview of private tennis clubs, with membership required.

7 Sailing
Blustery San Francisco Bay offers the perfect sailing conditions. On any sunny weekend, the waters are mottled with billowing sails. Charter a yacht or a masted schooner, take sailing lessons at Sailing San Francisco (sailingsanfrancisco. com), or tour the Bay on a motor cruiser, catamaran, or sailboat. Fun to watch

**Sailboats in the waters of
San Francisco Bay**

TOP 10
SPORTING TEAMS

1. Sacramento Kings
w nba.com/kings
Men's NBA basketball team. The
season runs from October to April.

2. San Francisco Giants
w mlb.com/giants
Baseball team, plays April to October.

3. Golden State Warriors
w nba.com/warriors
Popular NBA basketball team
nicknamed the "Dubs."

4. Golden State Valkyries
w valkyries.wnba.com
A WNBA team, the Valkyries made
their debut in spring 2025.

5. San Jose Earthquakes
w sjearthquakes.com
Men's Major League Soccer team.

6. Bay FC
w bayfc.com
A Bay Area women's soccer team
that debuted in 2024.

7. Napa Valley 1839 FC
w napavalley1839.com
Wine Country-based men's and
women's soccer club that competes
in the National Premier Soccer League
Golden Gate Conference.

8. Oakland Spiders
w oaklandspiders.com
Ultimate frisbee team in Oakland that
is part of the professional Ultimate
Frisbee Association.

9. San Jose Sharks
w nhl.com/sharks
The Bay Area's NHL ice-hockey team.

10. San Francisco 49ers
w 49ers.com
NFL team, plays September to January.

are the frequent regattas and boating
events, from Opening Day on the Bay
to Fleet Week and the Fourth of July.

8 Golf
Golf is a popular activity in the
Bay Area, with many courses scattered around the region. TPC Harding
Park *(tpc.com/hardingpark)* has been
revamped for professional tournaments,
and Presidio Golf Course *(presidiogolf.
com)* is among the best in the country.
Locals love Lincoln Park *(lincolnparkgolf
course.com)*, an affordable course above
Lands End; the par-3 Golden Gate Park
Golf Course *(goldengateparkgolf.com)*; and
the nine-hole Gleneagles Golf Course.

9 Kayaking
Unpredictable waters and winds
in the Bay call for a professional guide.
While sunset paddle tours are available
at Richardson Bay and Angel Island,
you can enjoy a calmer experience at
McCovey Cove.

10 Windsurfing
The Bay is one of the most
popular windsurfing and kiteboarding
sites in the world. Spectators often
watch from the shoreline, especially at
Crissy Field. Boardsports shops offer
lessons and rentals.

**Biking with the Golden Gate
Bridge in the backdrop**

San Francisco 49ers' stadium

OFF THE BEATEN PATH

1 Angel Island State Park
🕐 Sunrise–sunset daily
🌐 angelisland.com

Angel Island is reached by ferry from Tiburon (p132). This island once served as an immigration station, and has a dedicated museum on-site. Hiking trails loop the wooded island, rising to 776 ft (237 m) above sea level. The picnic tables on the lawns around Ayala Cove are perfect for soaking up views of the Bay, while on weekends, live music and draft beer make the deck at Angel Island Café a good place to hang out.

Enjoying a picnic and view of the Bay from Angel Island State Park

2 Yachting and Lawn Bowling in the Park
📍 B4 🏛 Golden Gate Park

For more than a century, members of the Lawn Bowling Club (sflbc.org) have welcomed spectators at their greensward. The steam-powered and electric sailing vessels of the Model Yacht Club (sfmyc.org) can be seen zooming across Spreckels Lake daily, particularly during the Wooden Boats on Parade event held every other year in the fall.

3 Tin How Temple
📍 N4 🏛 125 Waverly Place
🕐 9:30am–3pm Fri–Wed

On a Chinatown backstreet in a colorful 19th-century building, a narrow stairway leads past a mah-jongg parlor to the Tin How Temple, where incense wafts through a lantern-lit chamber dedicated to the Queen of Heaven.

4 San Francisco City Guides
📍 R2 🏛 SF Public Library, 100 Larkin St 🌐 sfcityguides.org

Founded by local librarians, the San Francisco City Guides offers a diverse range of seven different volunteer-led tours of the city. There's something for everyone, from art and history tours to film and literary ones. Though these are free, attendees are encouraged to tip the guides, all of whom are volunteers.

5 SS Jeremiah O'Brien
Ferrying troops and supplies during World War II, the SS *Jeremiah O'Brien (p27)* is one of only two restored survivors of the original 2,710 Liberty Ships. It also took part in the invasion of Normandy. Located on PIER 39, this 441-ft-(134-m-) long ship fires up her engines on "Steaming Weekends," and there are daily tours as well.

6 Sutro Baths
🔲 A3 📍 1004 Point Lobos Ave
🕐 Sunrise–sunset daily 🌐 nps.gov/places/000/sutro-baths.htm
These baths were once a saltwater bathing pool and the world's largest indoor swimming pool. Today, all that remains are atmospheric ruins in a wild and rocky setting. It's a great place to watch the rise and fall of the incoming tide as it fills and refreshes the water of the pools.

7 Gospel Music at Glide Memorial Church
Crowds gather on Sundays at 9am and 11am for the joyful sound of services at Glide Memorial United Methodist Church *(p55)*. With a 125-voice gospel choir singing jazz, blues, and rock and roll, plus an audience made up of all ages, races, and religions, the emotional scene is set for the compelling Marvin K. White, who welcomes all comers.

8 Lyon Street Steps
🔲 E2 📍 Lyon St at Broadway
Take your time climbing the Lyon Street steps adjacent to the Presidio (there are over 200) for sweeping, bird's-eye views of the Bay, the Presidio, the Palace of Fine Arts,

The steeply descending Lyon Street Steps

and the manicured gardens and balconied perfection of the Pacific Heights mansions. At the top, there is a gate into the Presidio.

9 Cottage Row
🔲 F3 📍 Between Sutter & Bush 📞 (415) 391-2000
🕐 Sunrise–sunset daily
A hidden gem, the historic Cottage Row mini-park is lined with late-1800s Italianate houses from the era of horse-drawn streetcars. Nearby, at Sutter Street, is the Issei Garden, honoring the first-generation Japanese immigrants who helped shape what is now Japantown.

10 Presidio Sculptures
🔲 D2 🌐 presidio.gov
The Presidio forest is home to sculptures by English artist Andy Goldsworthy. His first installation here, the impressive *Spire*, made of cypress trees, stands 100-ft (30-m) high, towering over a small grove. Another popular piece, *Wood Line*, stretches 1,200 ft (366 m) through the century-old eucalyptus groves, with its branches creating a zigzagging line that weaves through the forest.

FAMILY ATTRACTIONS

1 Children's Creativity Museum

This elaborate complex (p44) is part of the Yerba Buena Gardens. There's a carousel; a labyrinth; a studio where kids can script, produce, and star in their own videos; art studios; and a digital workshop. Suitable for those aged 2 to 12.

2 San Francisco Zoo

Kids will never forget their direct encounters with farm animals at this zoo (p124) and visits with baby animals, which may include gorillas, snow leopards, rhinos, or alpacas. Top-quality children's programs, many feeding times, and the creepy-crawly insect denizens, make it a must for budding zoologists.

3 Aquariums

Part of Golden Gate Park's California Academy of Sciences (p38), the Steinhart Aquarium is a big hit with kids. The darkened corridors are filled with glowing tanks, home to some of the weirdest creatures on the planet. There's also an educational tide pool for kids. At Fisherman's Wharf (p26), Aquarium of the Bay gives an even greater undersea experience, with walk-through transparent tunnels surrounded by sea life.

4 Randall Museum

E4 199 Museum Way, Buena Vista 10am–5pm Tue–Sat Mon & public hols randallmuseum.org

A small, welcoming complex, this museum has honeybees, a model train, the Natural Sciences Lab, a ceramic studio, and a high-tech STEM lab. There are also interactive desert, riparian, urban, and marine habitats.

5 Alcatraz Island

"The Rock" (p28) is always a hit with older children, particularly those who enjoy the grim aspects of the place. The island's natural beauty, as well as the ferry ride out and back, will also delight.

6 Bay Area Discovery Museum

557 McReynolds Rd, Sausalito 10am–4pm Wed–Sun Public hols & two weehs in Sep bayarea discoverymuseum.org

This hands-on museum on the Marin County waterfront is aimed at children aged six months to ten years. There's an art studio, a science lab, a workshop on "How Things Work," and a media center, along with year-round, STEAM-focused day camps.

The Tornado Exhibit at the Exploratorium

California Indian baskets
at the Randall Museum

7 Metreon
This shopping centre *(p44)* has an impressive IMAX 3D movie theater. Here, you can watch the latest Hollywood blockbusters with sound effects amped up to the highest level. The Metreon also offers several food court options and great views over the city from the fourth-floor deck.

8 Children's Fairyland
🏠 699 Bellevue Ave, Oakland
🕐 Hours vary, chech website
🌐 fairyland.org
Opened in 1948, this amusement park was the inspiration for Disneyland. It was designed for ages eight years and under and only admits adults accompanied by children.

9 Angel Island State Park
Angel Island *(p70)* is ideal for a family outing. You can picnic, swim, hike, kayak, camp, or take the tram tour that goes around the island, with a guide who points out sites of historic interest.

10 Exploratorium
At this science museum *(p95)*, kids can learn how their senses work, and also delve into the laws of physics through experiments, like making simple circuit boards. Reserve in advance for the Tactile Dome, in which you feel your way along in total darkness.

TOP 10 PLAYGROUNDS

1. Helen Diller Civic Center Playground
📍 R2 🏠 55 Larkin St
An award-winning playscape inspired by the city's weather patterns.

2. Alice Chalmers Playground
📍 N6 🏠 670 Brunswick St
This playground features a twisty high-tower slide.

3. Willie "Woo Woo" Wong Playground
📍 N4 🏠 830 Sacramento St
Named after a local basketball star, this urban park features sand-floor grounds, and a Chinese-zodiac theme.

4. Golden Gate Park 45th Avenue Playground
The "Blue Boat Playground" within the larger park *(p36)* has ocean-themed structures.

5. Lafayette Park
Dog-friendly park *(p62)* with pine and eucalyptus trees, tennis courts, and hilltop views of the city.

6. Joe DiMaggio Playground
📍 L3 🏠 651 Lombard St
North Beach park with athletic and bocce courts and large play structures. Bocce (an Italian version of lawn bowling) is played most afternoons on the public court.

7. Huntington Park
📍 N3 🏠 California St and Taylor St
On the site of Collis P. Huntington's mansion, atop posh Nob Hill, this park includes a stately fountain and a play area.

8. Alta Plaza Park
📍 E2 🏠 Jackson St and Steiner St
Concrete staircases crisscross this hilltop park and playground.

9. Presidio Wall Playground
📍 D2 🏠 Pacific St and Spruce St
With jungle gyms, a slide, and ball fields, this park has everything required for a day out.

10. South Park
📍 H3 🏠 64 S Park St
This park has a play structure inspired by designer Isamu Noguchi.

LOCAL DISHES

A Mission District sandwich on Dutch Crunch bread

1 Dutch Crunch Bread
Dutch Crunch bread (Dutch tiger bread) is a popular sandwich base, but visitors probably don't know how ubiquitous the crackly-topped, soft French roll is. Almost every sandwich shop offers it, and it's increasingly common to find at local grocery stores.

2 Burmese Tea Leaf Salad
San Francisco is the Burmese restaurant capital of the US, with at least a dozen in the city and more in the Bay Area. Tea leaf salad, or *lahpet thoke*, is a popular dish from Myanmar that combines tangy fermented tea leaves marinated in oil with salt, crunchy split peas, nuts, sesame seeds, dried ground shrimp, and fried garlic, in a fish-sauce-based dressing.

3 Dumplings
San Franciscans love dumplings and there are endless varieties available, from dim sum favorites like *har gow* (shrimp) and *siu mai* (pork and shrimp) to Nepalese *momos*. Popular dumplings include *xiao long bao* (soup dumplings), *sheng jian bao* (pan-fried soup dumplings), and boiled *jiaozi*.

4 Mission-style Burritos
A must-try for first-time visitors, this San Franciscan version of a Mexican favorite is a distinctively super-sized portable meal. A large flour tortilla (sometimes even two) encases meat, beans, and pico de gallo; popular add-ons include rice, cheese, sour cream, and avocado. Taqueria stalwarts claim to have invented the style in the 1960s, while other shop owners say "Mission-style" is purely marketing. Either way, the burritos are hugely delicious.

5 Irish Coffee
The Buena Vista *(p107)* in Fisherman's Wharf *(p26)* is credited with introducing Irish coffee to San Francisco and the US in 1952. Since then, the drink has become synonymous with the city, and bartenders make up to 2,000 a day. With precision, they dissolve sugar cubes in black coffee, add Irish whiskey, then gently float lightly whipped cream on top.

6 Cioppino
This flavorful seafood stew is a classic San Francisco dish. The story goes that in the 1990s, Italian fishers at Fisherman's Wharf would throw all of their catches of the day into a communal stew, yelling "Chip in!". This became cioppino, an Italian American stew now on menus throughout the city.

7 Garlic Noodles
Credit goes to Thanh Long *(thanhlongsf.com)* for inventing this Vietnamese American dish decades ago, and now it's standard across Vietnamese restaurant menus in the Bay Area. Chewy noodles (or even plain spaghetti) are mixed with plenty of garlic, butter, some combination of fish sauce, oyster sauce, and Maggi sauce, and parmesan cheese.

8 Dungeness Crab
With a sweet flavor and meaty texture, this seafood sends San Franciscans wild during Dungeness

Roasted Dungeness crab served whole

crab season, which runs roughly November to June. Find it at Fisherman's Wharf restaurants *(p107)* dressed in butter or in Italian cioppino stew, but also try other versions in the city, like roasted in garlic sauce or deep-fried salt-and-pepper style.

9 Joe's Scramble
A hearty dish ubiquitous on city diner menus, Joe's Scramble is scrambled eggs with spinach and ground beef. Common additions include onions, garlic, mushrooms, or shredded cheese. Origin stories range from it being a Gold Rush-era dish to a 1920s late-night invention for jazz musicians. What is safe to say is that Original Joe's *(originaljoes.com)* popularized the dish in 1937, and it's still on the menu there today.

10 Boba
Originally from Taiwan, boba drinks – chewy marble-sized tapioca balls in milk or fruit tea – began to show up at Chinese-run, family-owned stores in the late 1990s. A second wave was sparked by the arrival of Taiwanese boba chains, and now in its third wave, multi-generational Asian Americans are opening boba shops with a focus on local ingredients and fun flavors that include matcha, horchata, and more non-traditional drinks.

TOP 10 DESSERTS

Olallieberry pie with ice cream

1. Morning Bun
Tartine *(p121)* has the best version of this flaky, coiled pastry, but morning buns are a uniquely San Francisco treat.

2. Ice Cream Sundae
The city is full of ice cream parlors, but the San Franciscan way to eat it is as a sundae – multiple scoops drizzled with chocolate and a cherry on top.

3. Olallieberry Pie
This tart-but-sweet berry is only in season for a short time, but city bakeries make good use of it in pies.

4. Cruffin
Though invented in Australia, this hybrid breakfast pastry was made popular in San Francisco.

5. Zanze's Cheesecake
An iconic San Francisco dessert, this cheesecake is a must-try.

6. Donut
Donut shops are all over San Francisco, and you can't go wrong with any one you choose.

7. Fortune Cookies
Invented in San Francisco, Chinese fortune cookies are a city staple.

8. Dandelion Chocolate
Dandelion is a San Francisco specialty chocolate with different flavors on offer.

9. Coffee Crunch Cake
Invented in Japantown, this crunchy, coffee-flavored cake is a morning pick-me-up available across the city.

10. It's-it Ice Cream Sandwich
A city competitor to the sundae, this shop has sold its famous ice cream sandwiches since 1928.

CAFÉS AND BARS

Irish coffee being poured at The Buena Vista Café

1 The Buena Vista Café
The Buena Vista Café (p107) is always packed with customers who come for the good breakfasts and strong coffee. This friendly café claims to have been the first to introduce Irish coffee to America in 1952. First served at Shannon Airport in Ireland, the flavorful drink is composed of Irish whiskey, a sugar cube, hot coffee, and a foamy collar of whipped cream.

2 Specs' Twelve Adler Museum Café
With an exuberant atmosphere (p97), this bar is like a museum filled with

Beat memorabilia. The popular house drink here is the Jack Kerouac, which is a mix of rum, tequila, orange or cranberry juice, and lime.

3 Caffè Trieste
If you are interested in learning about the colorful history of this quarter, do not miss out on this North Beach landmark (p100). Whether it is from the literary and artistic point of view, or for the Italian culture, this place makes for a great experience. It's a great place for a cup of something warm, and to sit and people-watch or dip into one of San Francisco's free weekly newspapers.

4 Tartine Bakery and Café
You may find a line out the door at this purveyor of rustic breads (p121), "hot pressed" sandwiches, pizzas, cakes, and tarts. The co-owners have both been awarded the prestigious James Beard Award for Outstanding Pastry Chef.

5 Vesuvio Café
Since 1948, Vesuvio (p100) has been the North Beach haunt of artists, writers, and bon vivants of all stripes,

The lovely bar area at Vesuvio Café

many of whom wander across the street to the famous City Lights Bookstore (p98) and back.

6 Blue Bottle Café
This hip coffee roaster (p14) kicked off San Francisco's latest café trend; it serves up perfect cappuccinos and lattes in its chic, industrial SoMa space. Also on offer are Kyoto-style iced coffees, brewed using the Japanese slow-drip method. Perfection takes time, however, and these baristas take their work very seriously, so be prepared for a bit of a wait. The experience is worth trying at least once.

7 Arizmendi
This cooperative (p113) delights customers on both sides of the Bay with artisan breads, delicious morning pastries, and gourmet pizzas. The 9th Ave location is just a block from Golden Gate Park (p36).

8 One Market
Located just a few steps away from the Embarcadero (p120) and the waterfront, this lively bistro (p101) sets an atmosphere for fun. It offers California-style cuisine and the dishes are made from farm-fresh ingredients.

9 Bourbon & Branch
You'll need the nightly password to enter this classy bar (p120). Once inside, enjoy inventive cocktails in one of the most beautifully designed bars in the city, and explore the many secret rooms.

10 Absinthe
Established in 1988, this bistro (p113) is hugely popular with the locals. The menu here offers Parisian-style fare along with a wide selection of classic cocktails. Located adjacent to the bar is a private dining room, with an interior that captures *fin-de-siècle* France. Make sure to check out its incredible wine list.

TOP 10 BRUNCH VENUES

French toast with caramel

1. Mama's on Washington Square
📍 L4 🏠 1701 Stockton 🕐 Mon
The greatest French toast in town.

2. Sears Fine Food
This Union Square institution (p101) is noted for its silver dollar pancakes.

3. Plow
📍 H5 🏠 1299 18th St
Sample delights such as smoked trout toast and lemon ricotta pancakes.

4. Fable
📍 E5 🏠 558 Castro St
Enjoy pancakes and French toast with steak, eggs Benedict, and chilaquiles on a sunny patio at this place.

5. Kantine
📍 F4 🏠 1906 Market St 🕐 Mon
Scandinavian-style porridges, pastries and customizable brunch boards.

6. Presidio Social Club
📍 E2 🏠 563 Ruger St
An elegant restaurant serving up old-school drinks and brunch classics.

7. Just for You Café
📍 H5 🏠 732 22nd St
Soul-food-inspired brunch in the Dogpatch neighborhood.

8. Kate's Kitchen
📍 F4 🏠 471 Haight St
Huge portions of breakfast specialties, including a "French Toast Orgy."

9. Tosca Café
📍 G2 🏠 242 Columbus Ave
A good selection of bagels and French toasts topped with fruit.

10. St. Francis Fountain
📍 G5 🏠 2801 24th St
A charming, classic diner with wooden booths and a candy counter.

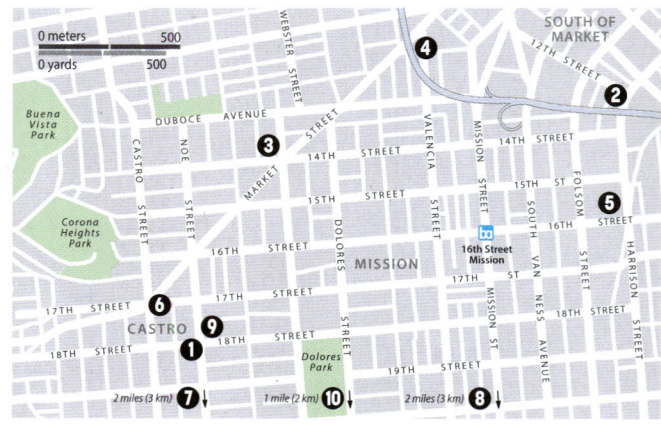

LGBTQ+ VENUES

Vintage car parked outside Moby Dick

1 Moby Dick
📍 E5 🏠 4049 18th St
📞 (415) 861-1199
This old-time Castro hangout attracts a more mature crowd. It's generally a bunch of regulars getting together to play pinball or pool. The music is largely 1980s retro, which sets a fun-loving tone.

2 SF Eagle
📍 G4 🏠 398 12th St 🌐 sf-eagle.com
Bikers and leather boys still rule at this venerable SoMa dive. Come here to revel in the beer-busting, sexually free atmosphere. The back patio comes alive with Sunday afternoon Beer Busts, and Thursdays feature live performances.

3 Churchill
📍 F4 🏠 198 Church St
🌐 churchillsf.com
Located in the Castro district, this cocktail bar is set in military barracks inspired by those used in World War II. It features vintage artifacts as well as pool tables, and serves top-notch cocktails in mason jars. It also offers fine wines and a variety of draft and bottled beers.

4 Martuni's
📍 F4 🏠 4 Valencia St at Market 📞 (415) 241-0205
With its decor of glass and chrome and the regulars' penchant for singing old torch songs, this is a very retro piano bar. Martuni's draws a mixture of drag queens and the larger LGBTQ+ community, Broadway fans, and anyone who likes a good singalong – or who doesn't mind embarrassing themselves on the microphone.

5 Jolene's
📍 G4 🏠 2700 16th St
🌐 jolenessf.com
An array of events takes place here: Western gear is encouraged

on Coyote Queer while Beso! is a queer Latin American party. The venue proudly welcomes the transgender and non-binary communities. On Sundays, there is the Drag & Burlesque Variety Show and brunch. Check the website for all the programs at this Mission District favorite.

6 Twin Peaks
P E5 **A** 401 Castro St
W twinpeakstavern.com
Conveniently located on the corner of Market Street, this legendary and distinctive tavern offers one of the best views of the Castro, whether by day or night. The interior is an inviting, pillowed triangular space with plate-glass windows.

7 Wild Side West
P G6 **A** 424 Cortland Ave
W wildsidewest.com
Founded in the 1960s, this laidback spot has a full bar inside, a patio area out back, and a beer garden. Take part in a game of pool or enjoy the flatscreens on game days. Trivia night is every Wednesday at 8pm.

8 Sundance Saloon
P G6 **A** 550 Barneveld Ave near Hwys 280 and 101 **W** sundance saloon.org
Don your Stetson and cowboy boots at this large country-and-western dance club. Two-step and linedance lessons are offered on Sundays and Thursdays. The saloon also hosts various special events.

9 Last Call Bar
P E5 **A** 3988 18th St
W thelastcallbar.com
Friendly, unpretentious dive bar with an Irish-pub-like atmosphere, complete with a jukebox, two large screens that cater to sports fans, and a cozy fireplace to keep warm on cold and foggy days. Happy hour begins at noon and lasts till 7pm every day.

10 El Rio
A delightful dive bar *(p119)* that features daily specials on drinks and free oysters on Fridays, and often hosts live events, from charity fundraisers to trivia to karaoke. There are plenty of other activities too, including shuffle-board and pool, plus ping-pong tables on the back patio.

Patrons enjoying a drink at the popular El Rio

NIGHTS OUT

1 Jazz Music
The Fillmore District was nicknamed the "Harlem of the West" for its booming jazz scene in the 1940s and 1950s. Clubs and venues in the Fillmore and nearby still echo that spirit, with places like Sheba Piano Lounge (*shebapianolounge. com*), Black Cat (*blackcatsf.com*), and The Royale (*p119*), along with the annual Fillmore Jazz Festival (*p89*).

2 Gold Rush Ghost Tours
Taking a nighttime ghost tour is a great way to learn about the city's Gold Rush and Wild West history. A once-lawless red-light district full of outlaws and gambling houses has left behind many harrowing tales. Try The Haunt (*thehauntghosttours.com*) or San Francisco Ghosts (*sfghosts.com*) for spooky and informative tours.

3 Beach Bonfires
During burn season (March–October), San Franciscans like to wind down the day with a sunset campfire at Ocean Beach (*p123*). There are communal fire rings near stairwells 15 to 20, and firewood and snacks are available at nearby shops. Ask to share a fire pit – and read up on the pit rules beforehand.

4 Unique Theater Shows
San Francisco has many cool theater venues offering everything from experimental multimedia shows to touring musicals. Geary Boulevard (*p110*) is at the center of the Theater District, but unique shows also take place at venues like the DNA Lounge (*p120*), Yerba Buena Center for the Arts (*p44*), and Gray Area (*grayarea.org*).

5 Late-Night Literature
As befits a city with such an illustrious literary heritage, San Francisco plays host to evening poetry events and book readings. The corner of 16th and Mission streets has a regular open-mic art event featuring poets, authors, and everything in between, while City Lights Bookstore (*p98*) holds evenings of book talks and readings. Bibliophiles also shouldn't miss the annual Litquake literary festival (*litquake.org*) each October.

6 Clubs
San Francisco has a pulsating after-hours scene, with a variety of late-night venues to spend a few hours dancing at a club. Most clubs are clustered in the SoMa district: Aunt Charlie's Lounge (*p119*) is a drag bar with a grungy vibe; the 500 Club (*p119*) is a local favorite; and you can't go wrong with El Rio (*p119*).

7 Comedy Shows
The city has many long-running comedy clubs, from Cobb's Comedy (*cobbscomedy.com*) to Punch Line (*p100*); several famous comedians, including Robin Williams, have honed their chops here. Check out regular

A performance in one of the city's jazz clubs

open-mic comedy nights in bars like Bimbo's 365 Club *(p100)* and places around North Beach to see the talent.

8 Dress up for the Opera
Get dressed up for a night (or two) and enjoy the oldest surviving ballet and opera companies on the West Coast. The San Francisco Ballet and San Francisco Opera both perform at the beautiful War Memorial Opera House *(p97)* and the performances are always a treat.

9 Alcatraz by Night
Alcatraz *(p28)* offers special tours that take you on a ferry ride to the island in the evening for beautiful sunset views. Tour companies like City Experiences *(cityexperiences.com)* offer dinner ferry cruises that show off the island and other Bay landmarks.

10 Bay Bridge Lights
Reopened in 2025 after a two-year hiatus, the Bay Lights *(p59)* along the San Francisco–Oakland Bay Bridge are now made up of 25,000 individual LED lights that change color, light up in time to music, and mark holidays and celebrations.

The San Francisco–Oakland Bay Bridge at sunset

TOP 10
BARS AND CLUBS

Outdoors at the Tonga Room

1. The Tonga Room and Hurricane Bar
This tiki bar *(p101)* has delivered Polynesian dazzlement since 1945.

2. The Great Northern
One of the few proper dance clubs in the city, this club *(p119)* is well known for its fun hip-hop shows.

3. DNA Lounge
The eclectic DNA Lounge *(p120)* has seven bars and four dance floors.

4. Bottom of the Hill
Open seven days a week in Potrero Hill, this *(p120)* is one of the best live-music venues in the city.

5. Boom Boom Room
🅥 F3 🅐 1601 Fillmore St
As popular for its great live blues, jazz, and funk, as it is for its welcoming mood, this club has a great energy.

6. Monarch
🅥 G3 🅐 101 6th St
Known for attracting great bands, Monarch is a premier nightclub.

7. Bodega
This wine bar *(p100)* has an excellent list of natural wines.

8. Make-Out Room
The Mission's favorite nightclub *(p119)*, this spot has live music, comedy, and literary events.

9. Bimbo's 365 Club
Whether you are into swing, jazz, or rock, this San Francisco institution *(p100)* delivers.

10. Punch Line Comedy Club
There is no better venue for a laugh than this comedy club *(p100)*.

STORES AND SHOPPING CENTERS

1 Green Apple Books
This beloved independent bookstore *(p126)*, located in the Richmond neighborhood, has a great selection of both new and secondhand books. There's also another branch at the SFO airport, convenient for picking up some in-flight entertainment.

2 Neiman Marcus
P4 **150 Stockton St**
After some retail therapy at the designer clothing store, Neiman Marcus, grab a quick bite in the Fresh Market, or linger at The Rotunda for fine dining, or high tea, under the stained-glass dome, while admiring the views.

3 Wilkes Bashford
This luxury clothing store *(p118)* features high-end designers with a bent for fashionable clothing and footwear. It has great options for the denizens of the Financial District.

4 Ferry Building Marketplace
Wander through one of the world's greatest gourmet food markets *(p52)* and stop to taste fresh oysters, Vietnamese or Mexican food, salumi, Blue Bottle coffee, pastries, chocolates, and cheesecake. There is a farmers' market on Tuesday, Thursday, and Saturday in front of the Ferry Building, set along the Embarcadero.

5 Amoeba Music
Situated along Haight Street, Amoeba Music *(p112)* is the world's largest indie music store, with several other locations in California. It stocks LPs, tapes, as well as CDs and evokes a true sense of the past. Also on sale here are a vast selection of DVDs, apparel, and posters, plus plenty of branded items from the store.

6 Timbuk2
F3 **506 Hayes St**
A brand synonymous with the city's casual backpack culture, Timbuk2 is famous for its ever-changing collection of messenger bags, backpacks, and other bags and cases.

7 Saks Fifth Avenue
P4 **384 Post St**
For decades, the name Saks has been synonymous with high style,

Food stalls at the Ferry Building Marketplace

Clothing on display at the popular Saks Fifth Avenue store

and this branch of the New York mainstay is one of the best embodiments of the store's mythic élan. Visits to the store are by appointment only, with a personal assistant accompanying you as you browse.

8 Embarcadero Center
⊞ N6 🏠 Embarcadero & Battery, Sacramento & Clay sts
Four high-rise blocks connect to form this sprawling shopping center, conveniently located in FiDi. Here, you'll find a mix of chain stores like Sephora and small local vendors participating in the city's "Vacant to Vibrant" pilot program, which transforms empty downtown spaces into food and retail outlets.

9 Ghirardelli Square
⊞ K1 🏠 900 North Point St
Housing about 20 restaurants and stores, this former chocolate factory has become one of the most frequented destinations in Fisherman's Wharf (p26). The stores range from tourist T-shirt shops to fine jewelry boutiques.

10 San Francisco Centre
⊞ Q4 🏠 865 Market St
This huge center has ten levels and nearly 400 stores, including Bath and Body Works, Zara, and Bloomingdale's, as well as a movie theater, a food court, and many fine restaurants and cafes.

TOP 10
SHOPPING AREAS

1. Grant Avenue
⊞ N4
Chic shopping off Union Square, Chinatown emporiums, and North Beach hangouts in Upper Grant.

2. Union Street
The converted Victorian homes here (p109) house an assortment of stores.

3. Union Square
Traditionally the focal point of all the best stores (p97), including Tiffany & Co, Armani, Cartier, Gucci, and Chanel.

4. Upper Fillmore Street
⊞ E2
A colorful choice of cafés, restaurants, and boutiques, all geared toward a high-end Pacific Heights clientele.

5. Market Street
⊞ Q3
Market Street is a bustling shopping hub, with a massive IKEA and an impressive food hall.

6. Hayes Valley
These blocks offer galleries and stores with an avant-garde feel (p110).

7. Chestnut Street
⊞ K1
Clothing boutiques, health-food stores, and an old-fashioned cinema.

8. The Mission District
Plenty of discount stores and funky home-furnishing shops (p116).

9. Castro Street
Fine shops, LGBTQ+ bookstores and erotic boutiques (p115).

10 Haight Street
The place (p111) for secondhand clothing, emporiums, and shoe stores.

Posters for sale on Grant Avenue

SAN FRANCISCO FOR FREE

1 Waterfront Ramble
There is a lot to enjoy for free along the waterfront. Listen to *The Wave Organ,* an acoustic wave-activated sculpture at 83 Marina Green Drive, peruse murals in the Maritime Museum *(p56),* watch sea lions at PIER 39 *(p26),* or bask in the misty Fog Bridge installation at the Exploratorium *(p95).*

2 Outdoor Summer Concerts
⌂ Sigmund Stern Recreation Grove at 19th Ave & Sloat Blvd
Ⓦ sterngrove.org
Pines and eucalyptus create a verdant backdrop for the amphitheater where the free Stern Grove Festival concerts take place on summer Sundays from June to August. Many picnic while enjoying jazz, rock, the symphony, ballet, and opera.

3 Bayside View of the San Francisco Giants
Ⓟ H3 ⌂ McCovey Cove off Giants Promenade
During baseball season, it's free to watch the San Francisco Giants play at home in Oracle Park from the Giants Promenade walkway at what is known as the "Viewing Point."

4 Golden Gate Park
This 1.5-sq-mile (4-sq-km) urban garden *(p36)* is a great place to watch tai chi classes, swing dancing, or even bison roaming in their paddock. The Music Concourse hosts free concerts in summer, including the annual Opera in the Park *(sfopera.com)* event.

5 Fort Point National Historic Site
Situated at the foot of the Golden Gate Bridge, this fortress *(p53)* was built in 1861 to protect the city of San Francisco from Confederate attacks that never came. Children in particular love to see the cannons being loaded, as well as the semi-annual Civil War reenactments.

6 Guided Walking Tours
Dozens of daily, free walking tours are led by savvy locals and historians of SF City Guides *(p70),* giving insights into Coit Tower murals, Chinatown alleys, the LGBTQ+ Castro neighborhood, Victorian architecture, the Gold Rush, and other topics.

7 Free Museum Days
The first Tuesday of every month, museums open their doors for free, including the de Young Museum *(p40)* and the European-art-filled Legion of Honor *(p123).* The San Francisco Museum of Craft and Design *(p57)* has pay-what-you-can Wednesdays, and admission is free at the Museum of African Diaspora *(p44)* every first Saturday. Set in a stunning Beaux Arts edifice, the Asian Art Museum *(p56)* has free admission every first Sunday.

Grand Staircase at the San Francisco City Hall

The Wave Organ by Peter
Richards and George Gonzalez

8 The Presidio
Take a ranger-led tour to
experience centuries of military
history, from Spanish cannons to Civil
War barracks (*p104*). The Officers' Club
(*presidioofficersclub.com*) also runs
free cultural events. Meander the
forest trails and enjoy a picnic on
the beach or in the cozy, green,
seaview meadows.

9 Golden Gate Bridge
Whether under cloudy or sunny
skies, a walk or cycle across the
"international orange" Golden Gate
Bridge (*p22*) is a pleasure. The iconic
symbol of the city towers 260 ft
(79 m) above churning Bay waters, and
offers great views of Alcatraz Island,
sailboats, freighters, and ferries.

10 City Hall
Wander through the 1915
Beaux Arts City Hall, situated in the
Civic Center (*p97*), which houses city
government and public art. Tour
guides tell captivating stories of the
city's glory days and tragedies, such
as the 1906 earthquake and the assass-
ination of Mayor George Moscone
in 1978.

TOP 10
BUDGET TIPS

Hardly Strictly Bluegrass festival

1. One of the largest multi-genre
music festivals in the country, three-
day Hardly Strictly Bluegrass (*hardly
strictlybluegrass.com*) is free to all.

2. Go San Francisco (*gocity.com*)
Card holders get free or discounted
admission to more than 25 attractions, tours, and cruises.

3. Visit California's SF Welcome Center
(*visitcalifornia.com*) to book discounted
tickets for popular attractions.

4. TodayTix (*todaytix.com*) is an
online platform offering discounted
last-minute theater tickets.

5. Self-cater and picnic with
locally sourced food from the city's
world-famous farmers' markets
(*cdfa.ca.gov*).

6. Happy-hour bar menus of small
plates and discounted drinks are
available from about 4pm to 7pm.

7. Discount coupons and special
offers are available on the San
Francisco Travel website (*sftravel.
com/attraction-passes*).

8. At some Mexican places in the
Mission, delicious burritos and tacos
are less than $10. Sandwiches, pizza,
and hole-in-the-wall gems also are
good value.

9. Muni has one-, three-, and
seven-day passes with great savings.
These passes can be loaded onto a
Clipper card – either physical or
digital – along with cash funds
and are accepted across the Bay
Area transport systems (*p141*).

10. The FunCheap website (*sf.fun
cheap.com*) lists up-to-date free and
inexpensive activities and events.

Sea lions relaxing at PIER 39

FESTIVALS AND PARADES

1 Lunar New Year
Jan or Feb

Among the biggest Lunar New Year celebrations outside Asia, the festivities incorporate traditional displays and the parade of dragons, lions, and performers that winds through the streets of Downtown and Chinatown.

2 St. Patrick's Day Parade
Sat before Mar 17

With San Francisco's large Irish population, not to mention the 25 or so Irish pubs scattered around town, the St. Patrick's Day Parade and the revelry that continues into the night is one of the city's largest celebrations. The parade journeys from 2nd and Market Streets to the Civic Center.

3 Cherry Blossom Festival
Two weekends in Apr

Japantown (p109) comes to life spectacularly when the cherry trees blossom during April. There are displays of traditional arts and crafts, *taiko* drumming, martial arts demonstrations, and dancing, as well as delicious Japanese food.

4 Cinco de Mayo
Sat or Sun around May 5

Commemorating the French army defeat by General Ignacio Zaragoza in 1862 at Puebla, Mexico, this is one of the Latin American community's biggest annual festivals, featuring parades, fireworks, music, and dancing. In addition to the Civic Center, much of the fun happens in the Mission District.

5 Carnaval
Last weekend in May

Billed as the largest multicultural celebration on the West Coast, this festival, over 45 years old, celebrates the rich Latino, Caribbean, and African diasporic traditions of the Mission District and the San Francisco Bay Area. Groups work all year long, with the help of municipal grants, to create their dazzling costumes and put together their infectiously rhythmic routines.

6 San Francisco Pride
Sat & Sun in late Jun

More than 500,000 people attend this amazing LGBTQ+ event, the largest of its kind in the US, that takes over Market Street, from the Civic Center

Dressed in traditional Mexican attire during Cinco de Mayo

to the Embarcadero. Expect Dykes on Bikes®, the Sisters of Perpetual Indulgence, LGBTQ+ marching bands, muscle men, and much more. The floats – as well as the cheering throngs – are likely to be the most colorful, vivacious things you will see any time of the year in the city.

7 Stern Grove Festival
Sun, early Jun–late Aug

A much-loved San Francisco tradition, this festival (*p84*) showcases every kind of music in an idyllic atmosphere.

8 Fillmore Jazz Festival
Early Jul

This multiday festival celebrates the jazz heritage of the Fillmore district and San Francisco. The line-up always includes plenty of live music, along with a variety of vendors and crafts.

9 Independence Day
Jul 4

This festival, held from Aquatic Park to PIER 39, involves live entertainment, food stalls, and fireworks launched from several points along the Bayfront.

10 Fleet Week
Oct

At this celebration of US naval forces, air shows, and a parade of ships sail into the Bay with the spectacular San Francisco skyline as a backdrop.

Dragon dance performance during Lunar New Year

TOP 10 FAIRS AND GATHERINGS

1. Tet Festival
Jan–Feb
A multicultural party, but mainly Vietnamese American in theme.

2. Bay to Breakers
Late May
Runners race in funny costumes from the Ferry Building to Ocean Beach.

3. Native Contemporary Arts Festival
Jun
Featuring vendors, arts and crafts, spoken word, and music, this festival celebrates contemporary Indigenous cultures.

4. Haight-Ashbury Street Fair
Jun
You'll see that hippiedom is still alive and well after attending this fair.

5. North Beach Festival
Jun
The city's oldest street fair features arts and crafts and some great Italian food.

6. Sunset Night Market
Aug & Sep
This street fest on the west side features excellent food stalls.

7. Folsom Street Fair
Last Sun Sep
One of the biggest events for the LGBTQ+ and BDSM communities after Pride.

8. The Portola Festival
Late Sep
Indie and electronic music reign supreme at this festival.

9. Castro Street Fair
Early Oct
Founded by the late Harvey Milk to celebrate queer-owned businesses and the vitality of the Castro.

10. Halloween
Oct 31
Costumes and makeup are the highlight at this lively Castro party and parade.

DAY TRIPS FROM THE CITY

style residential gardens in the US. A beautiful park and a traditional teahouse are just two of its highlights.

3 Wine Country
Taking at least a day to drive up into the Napa and Sonoma valleys (p46) should be on everyone's San Francisco to-do list. Not only is the countryside beautiful, but also you can sample some of the best wines in the world. Dip into the restorative volcanic hot springs, and enjoy lavish spa treatments.

4 Stanford University
Located in the city of Palo Alto, with a Caltrain station right at the main gates, the palm-lined beauty of this campus (p136) makes it worth a trip. The motif of sandstone and red-tile roofs has been carried forward since the Romanesque Main Quadrangle was built in the late 1800s. The carvings on the arches and pillars set off the elaborate mosaic that graces the facade of the Memorial Church.

5 Half Moon Bay
This charming Victorian-era town is fringed with long, sandy beaches

1 Big Basin Redwoods State Park
⏱ 8am–sunset daily 🌐 parks.ca.gov ↗
Highway 9 is one of the most picturesque drives in the Bay Area, winding among green mountains and through little towns on the way to this park, which, although just a short drive from Silicon Valley, has a backwoods feel to it.

2 Los Gatos and Saratoga
In the hills above Silicon Valley, and below the Santa Cruz Mountains, these historic small towns offer charming shops, restaurants, and inns (p134). A top attraction in this area is a visit to the Hakone Gardens (hakone.com). Recognized as one of the National Trust for Historic Preservation's most notable sites, these gardens – built in 1917 – are among the oldest Japanese-

that are perfect for strolling and surfing. Half Moon Bay State Beach is actually made up of 3 miles (5 km) of adjacent beaches, alongside which the Coastside Trail runs. The local flower farms and busy fishing port are photogenic, while fresh seafood, art galleries, and country stores add to the mix.

6 Santa Cruz

This beach resort *(p134)* has always had a reputation for the vibrancy of its countercultural way of life. Along the beautiful coastline, the most prominent feature is the boardwalk's Giant Dipper Roller Coaster, which has been thrilling Santa Cruzers since 1924. The best swimming in the Bay Area is also here.

7 Sonoma Coast

About an hour's scenic drive from the city are sandy beaches, rocky coves, and the fisher village of Bodega Bay. From the deck or a window table at the Tides Wharf seafood restaurant *(835 Coast Highway One)*, watch harbor seals play and fishers unload their catches, then take a drive along world-famous Highway 1, stopping off at Sonoma Coast beaches.

8 Point Reyes

Some 110 sq miles (285 sq km) of pristine natural coastline make this promontory *(p134)* a haven for all sorts of wildlife and a thing of unforgettable, windswept beauty. You can watch whales and sea lions from Point Reyes Lighthouse.

Hiking the Ben Johnson trail in Muir Woods

9 Muir Woods National Monument

⏰ 8am–sunset daily 🌐 nps.gov/muwo 🔗

Named after the 19th-century conservationist John Muir *(p53)*, this 1-sq-mile (2-sq-km) woodland is home to some of the last-remaining first-growth redwood trees in the US. Some of these giants are over 1,000 years old and make for a towering backdrop to hikes throughout the forest. As parking is limited and fills up most days, reservations are required for vehicles and the Muir Woods Shuttle (gomuirwoods.com).

10 Monterey Peninsula

Day-trippers head to Monterey for its world-class aquarium, to shop and eat on Cannery Row (made famous by John Steinbeck), and to ramble along the shores of Point Lobos State Natural Reserve. Carmel-by-the-Sea is full of quaint cottages, art galleries, and boutique shops, as well as having a picturesque beach. Golfers make pilgrimages to visit the legendary Pebble Beach and Spanish Bay golf clubs, and to play at Bayonet Black Horse and Pacific Grove courses.

Stunning coastline of Point Reyes

AREA BY AREA

Grant Avenue in San Francisco's Chinatown

DOWNTOWN

The Downtown area may be small, but it is incredibly diverse, home to some of the city's oldest and newest landmarks. Here you'll find colorful Chinatown, exuberant North Beach, posh Nob and Russian hills, the bustling Financial District, the graceful Ferry Building, and the culture and Beaux Arts-style architecture of the Civic Center – all these and more are packed into the city's heart. This is also where you can ride the cable cars' most scenic routes, enjoying stunning views of the city. The cars will take you up Telegraph Hill, one of San Francisco's original "Seven Hills," where Coit Tower stands as one of the city's best-loved landmarks, competing with the Transamerica Pyramid not very far away.

Top 10 Sights
p95

Places to Eat
p101

Shops
p99

Cafés and Bars
p100

North Beach Sights
p98

For places to stay in this area, see p148

Street in Chinatown decorated with traditional Chinese lanterns

1 Chinatown

Since its beginnings in the 1850s, this densely populated neighborhood *(p32)* has held its own powerful cultural identity despite every threat and cajolery. Strolling through its bustling, narrow streets and alleys feels like stepping into a vibrant city within the city.

2 North Beach
⬛ L4

This lively neighborhood is the original "Little Italy" of the city, and is still noted for its great Italian restaurants and cafés, mostly lined up along and near Columbus Avenue. In the 1950s, it was also a magnet for the Beat writers and poets, notably Jack Kerouac and Allen Ginsberg *(p60)*, who brought to the area an alternative style that it still sports today. This is a great place for nightlife, from the tawdry bawdiness of Broadway strip joints to the simple pleasures of listening to a mezzo-soprano while you sip your cappuccino.

3 Nob Hill
⬛ N3

With the advent of the cable car, the highest hill in San Francisco was quickly populated with the elaborate mansions of local magnates – in particular, the "Big Four" who built the Transcontinental Railroad *(p96)* – and the name Nob Hill became synonymous with wealth and power. The 1906 earthquake, however, left only one "palace" standing, now the Pacific Union Club, which still proudly dominates the center of the summit. Today, instead of private mansions, Nob Hill is home to the city's fanciest hotels and apartment buildings, as well as Grace Cathedral.

4 Grace Cathedral
⬛ N3 🏛 1100 California St
🕐 10am–5pm Mon–Sat, 1–5pm Sun 🌐 gracecathedral.org

Inspired by French Gothic architecture, with dazzling stained-glass windows and towers topping 170 ft (50 m), this Episcopal cathedral is a photogenic landmark on Nob Hill.

5 Exploratorium
⬛ L6 🏛 Pier 15, Embarcadero
🕐 Museum: 10am–5pm Tue–Sat, noon–5pm Sun 🌐 exploratorium.edu 🔗

One of the world's first hands-on science museums, the Exploratorium now stands in a spectacular location on Pier 15. There are close to 1,000 exhibits spread among themed indoor galleries and a large outside space. There are also educational programs, a theater, an interactive gift shop, a Bay observatory, an outdoor plaza, two restaurants, and cafés. The museum has net-zero energy goals.

6 Financial District
M5

Montgomery Street, now the heart of the Financial District, was once lined with small stores where miners came to weigh their gold dust. It marks the old shoreline of shallow Yerba Buena Cove, which was filled in during the Gold Rush to create more land. Today it is lined with banking "temples" of the early 20th century and modern fabrications of glass and steel. At the end of Market Street stands the Ferry Building, which handled 100,000 commuters per day before the city's bridges were constructed, and is now a bustling meeting spot with cafés and artisan food shops. Its tower is inspired by the Moorish belfry of Seville Cathedral in Spain.

7 Jackson Square
M5

This neighborhood by the Transamerica Pyramid *(p55)* contains some of the city's oldest buildings. In the 19th century, it was notorious for its squalor, and was nicknamed the "Barbary Coast," but brothels and drinking establishments have given way to offices and antiques shops. The blocks around Jackson Street and Hotaling Place feature many original facades.

8 Russian Hill
M2

Another of San Francisco's precipitous heights, one side of Russian Hill is so steep you'll find no street at all, only steps. The most famous feature of this hill is the charming Lombard Street switchback – "The World's Crookedest Street" – which attests to the hill's notoriously unmanageable inclines. As with Nob Hill, with the cable car's advent, Russian Hill was claimed by the wealthy, and it maintains a lofty position in San Francisco society to this day. It supposedly took its name from the burial place of Russian fur traders, who were among the first Europeans to ply their trade at this port in the early 1800s.

Powell-Hyde cable car at Union Square

9 Union Square
P4

This important square, which gets its name from the pro-Union rallies held here in the early 1860s, received a $25-milion makeover in the early 2000s, which included the addition of performance spaces and grassy terraces. It is now the center for high-end shopping. With the Financial District on one side and the Theater District on the other, it is most picturesque along Powell Street, where the cable cars pass in front of the historic Westin St. Francis hotel. Its central column is dedicated to Admiral George Dewey and commemorates his victory in the Battle of Manila Bay during the Spanish-American War of 1898.

10 Civic Center
R1

The city's elaborate Beaux Arts administrative center includes the grand City Hall, the War Memorial Opera House, the Louise M. Davies Symphony Hall, the Herbst Theatre, the State Building, and the Main Library. The old Main Library was re-inaugurated as the stellar Asian Art Museum *(p56)* in 2003. The much grittier Tenderloin district is directly to the north, and the charming Hayes Valley *(p110)* is just southwest.

Famous Lombard Street on Russian Hill

A WALK AROUND NORTH BEACH

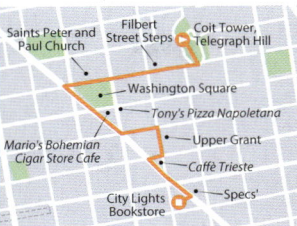

Morning

Starting at the top of North Beach, on **Telegraph Hill** *(p98)*, admire the famous views and visit **Coit Tower** *(p98)*, making sure to take in the murals. Next, walk down to **Filbert Street Steps** *(p98)* and go right a couple of blocks until you get to the lovely **Washington Square** *(p98)*, where, at the Catholic **Saints Peter and Paul Church** *(p98)*, Marilyn Monroe and local baseball great Joe DiMaggio had their wedding pictures taken. Continue on and pay a visit to **Mario's Bohemian Cigar Store Cafe** *(mariosbohem ian.com)*, where you can indulge in a bit of people-watching. Or, just behind on Stockton Street, head to **Tony's Pizza Napoletana** *(tonys pizzanapoletana.com)*, for some award-winning pizza.

Afternoon

After lunch, take a left on Green Street and go over one block to **Upper Grant** *(p98)*, with its funky shops and bars, a regular hangout since the 1950s. Turn right on to Vallejo Street, where a visit to the famous **Caffè Trieste** *(p100)* for a coffee and the artistic atmosphere is a must. Continue to **Specs'** *(specsbarsf.com)*, an exuberant bar filled with Beat memorabilia. Finally, just across Columbus is the immortal **City Lights Bookstore** *(p98)*, where you can browse Beat poetry by founder Lawrence Ferlinghetti and friends.

North Beach Sights

1. Coit Tower
📍 L5

The frescoes in this tower were painted by local artists in 1934, to provide jobs during the Depression. The murals offer sociopolitical commentary and details of life in California at the time.

2. North Beach Views

The panoramic views from both the hill and the top of the Coit Tower are justly celebrated. The wide arc sweeping from the East Bay and the Bay Bridge to Alcatraz and the Golden Gate Bridge is breathtaking.

3. Telegraph Hill
📍 L5

Named after the semaphore installed on its crest in 1850. The hill's eastern side was dynamited to provide rocks for landfill. Steps descend its slopes, lined with gardens. At its summit is Coit Tower.

4. Upper Grant
📍 L4

Saloons, cafés, and bluesy music haunts give this northerly section of Grant Avenue a very alternative feel.

**Neo-Gothic interior of the
Saints Peter and Paul Church**

5. City Lights Bookstore
**📍 M4 🏠 261 Columbus Ave
🌐 citylights.com**

The Beat poet Lawrence Ferlinghetti founded City Lights in 1953. It's a great place to leaf through poetry or the latest releases, or attend a reading or book launch in the evening.

6. Filbert Street Steps
📍 L5

The flowery descent down these steps provides great Bay views.

7. Broadway
📍 M5

Made famous in the 1960s for its various adult entertainments. The offerings haven't changed much, though today many venues are more mainstream.

8. Caffè Trieste

If you're in the neighborhood on a Saturday afternoon, don't miss the spirited jazz that takes place here *(p100)*. It is one of the longest-running musical shows in the city.

9. Washington Square
📍 L4

This pretty park is lined with Italian bakeries, restaurants, and bars. Don't be surprised to see practitioners of tai chi on the lawn every morning.

10. Saints Peter and Paul Church
**📍 L4 🏠 666 Filbert St
🕐 7:30am–4pm daily (to 1pm
public hols) 🌐 salesiansspp.org**

This Neo-Gothic church has an Italianesque facade, with an interior notable for its many columns and ornate altar. It is also known as the Italian Cathedral and the Fisherman's Church, names given as a result of the many Italian worshippers who originally lived in the neighborhood and made their living by fishing.

Shops

**Italian goods on display
at Molinari Delicatessen**

1. Molinari Delicatessen
📍G2 🏠373 Columbus Ave
🌐themolinarideli.com
Part of the neighborhood's
Italian American heritage, Molinari's
has been in business since 1896.
Stop by for excellent sandwiches,
fresh ravioli, whole salami, Italian
soft drinks, and other delights.

2. Lola of North Beach
📍K2 🏠900 North Point St
🌐lolaofnorthbeach.com
A charming souvenir store,
Lola of North Beach features
a massive collection of trinkets
and cards that are uniquely San
Franciscan. Ever-popular items
include a selection of enamel
pins and vibrant stickers.

3. Goorin Bros.
📍L4 🏠1612 Stockton St
🌐goorin.com
One of the city's finest hat shops
prides itself on offering excellent
service. Most of the custom hats
are handmade in the US.

4. Biordi Art Imports
📍M4 🏠412 Columbus Ave
🌐biordi.com
Known for its excellent Italian
ceramics, glass, and fine art, this
store imports its products from Italy
working directly with artisans.

5. Little Vine
📍P4 🏠1541 Grant Ave
🌐littlevine.mypreview.site
Grab one of the sandwich specials
sold here while browsing this quaint,
European-inspired shop, filled with
independently produced wines,
artisan cheeses, pickles, and
locally sourced honey.

6. XOX Truffles
📍L3 🏠754 Columbus Ave
🌐xoxtruffles.com
Enter a chocolate wonderland and
sample some of the finest truffles in
the city. There are also vegan varieties.

7. AB Fits
📍L4 🏠1519 Grant Ave
🌐abfits.com
This high-quality denim shop
has earned a cult following during
its many years in business. Over time,
it has expanded its range to include
shirts, outerwear, and accessories.

8. Knitz and Leather
📍L4 🏠1453 Grant Ave
📞(415) 583-3926
This small and chic shop sells ready-to-
wear items, as well as leather goods
handmade to order.

9. Macchiarini Creative Design
📍G2 🏠1544 Grant Ave
🌐macreativedesign.com
The oldest ongoing arts design
house, production studio, and gallery
in the entirety of the US, this shop has
been handcrafting individually made
sculptures and jewelry since 1948.

10. William Stout Architectural Books
📍M4 🏠804 Montgomery St
🌐stoutbooks.com
A landmark for design buffs all
over the world, this small shop
is divided into two spaces, with
newer books on display upstairs.

Quirky exterior of Vesuvio Café

Cafés and Bars

1. Caffè Trieste
M4 609 Vallejo St
(415) 982-2605
One of the city's most popular cafés, rich with an arty sense of nonchalance.

2. Tosca Cafe
M4 242 Columbus Ave
toscacafe-sf.com
Tosca has been renowned for its boozy, chocolate cappuccinos since it opened in 1919.

3. Punch Line Comedy Club
M5 444 Battery St
punchlinecomedyclub.com
Performances by talented local and national comedians will leave you in splits at this venue.

4. Tony Nik's Cafe
L4 1534 Stockton St
tonyniks.com
This long-established spot has a casual, retro vibe and is famous for its cold martinis and classic cocktail menu.

5. The Cheese School
F1 2535 3rd St
thecheeseschool.com
Learn how to make different cheeses and create your own charcuterie plate here. You can also try superb cheese boards and other snacks.

6. The Tonga Room and Hurricane Bar
N3 Fairmont Hotel, 950 Mason St Mon & Tue
fairmont-san-francisco.com
A tiki lounge that offers tropical tunes and yummy cocktails.

7. Bodega
Q3 138 Mason St
bodegasf.com
This stylish wine bar with modern decor offers a good selection of natural wines and small bites.

8. Vesuvio Café
M4 255 Columbus Ave
vesuvio.com
This North Beach mainstay serves potent drinks and is close to the City Lights Bookstore (*p98*).

9. Bimbo's 365 Club
K3 1025 Columbus Ave
bimbos365club.com
Around since 1931, Bimbo's features live music, comedy, and iconic holiday parties.

10. Press Club
P4 20 Yerba Buena Lane at Market (415) 744-5000
This popular and ultramodern lounge offers a wide selection of wines.

Places to Eat

1. Kokkari Estiatorio

M6 ⌂ 200 Jackson St
☎ (415) 981-0983 · $$$

The Greek cuisine here is a delectable revelation of flavors. The lamb shank and grilled octopus are not to be missed.

2. Golden Boy Pizza

L4 ⌂ 542 Green St
ⓦ goldenboypizza.com · $

At the locally popular hangout spot Golden Boy, the pioneers of Italian American-fusion-style pizza, you can enjoy your pie by the slice or by the pan. Each pizza is made with light focaccia instead of a more traditional-style dough.

3. One Market

N6 ⌂ 1 Market St at Steuart
☎ (415) 777-5577 🗓 Sat & Sun · $$

The views of the Bay's lights from here are spectacular at night. Enjoy the farm-fresh food.

4. Sears Fine Food

P4 ⌂ 439 Powell St
ⓦ searsfinefood.com · $

This 1950s retro coffee shop is famous for its breakfasts, and is always a reliable choice for a quick fill-up.

5. Quince

M5 ⌂ 470 Pacific Ave 🚇 L
ⓦ quincerestaurant.com · $$$

The tasting menu made with local ingredients has earned rave reviews for this Michelin-starred restaurant.

6. Lers Ros Thai

K2 ⌂ 730 Larkin St ⓦ lersros.com · $

This restaurant lives up to its name – in Sanskrit, "lers" translates as "excellent" and "ros" means "taste."

PRICE CATEGORIES

For a three-course meal for one with half a bottle of wine (or equivalent meal), taxes, and extra charges.

$ under $50 $$ $50–$100
$$$ over $100

---

7. Trestle

M5 ⌂ 531 Jackson St
ⓦ trestlesf.com · $$

A cozy little bistro with a welcoming vibe, Trestle offers an elegant three-course prix fixe menu.

8. Sotto Mare

L4 ⌂ 552 Green St
ⓦ sottomaresf.com · $$

Housed in a 19th-century building on a busy North Beach street, Sotto Mare serves Italian seafood dishes. Don't miss the crab cioppino (p74).

9. Tadich Grill

N5 ⌂ 240 California St
ⓦ tadichgrillsf.com · $$

This traditional restaurant serves classics such as clam chowder. Brusque staff add some fun to the atmosphere.

10. Yank Sing

H2 ⌂ 101 Spear St
ⓦ yanksing.com · $$

Endorsed by both Michelin and the James Beard organization, Yank Sing is one of the city's finest dim sum restaurants and the only one offering daily cart service.

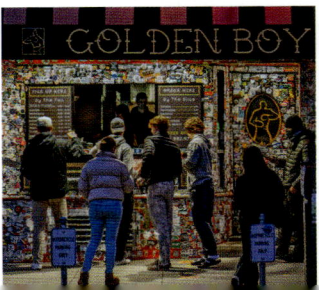

Patrons outside at
Golden Boy Pizza

THE NORTH SHORELINE

San Francisco began to grow along the north shoreline when the Spanish set up a military outpost at the Presidio in 1776. Today the shoreline is a showcase of both historical and modern attractions. The Palace of Fine Arts recalls the 1915 Panama-Pacific International Exposition; the vintage homes of the Marina District have stellar Bay views; ships depart from Pier 41 for Bay cruises; and tourists crowd the stores and seafood restaurants of Fisherman's Wharf.

Strolling the waterfront promenade at the Embarcadero

1 The Embarcadero
G1

Skirted with palm trees, the Embarcadero runs from the north shoreline down to the coast of Downtown, from Pier 45 to the San Francisco Giants' Oracle Park. It is lined with attractions and departure points for cruise ships. The Alcatraz Landing is at Pier 33 and Hornblower Cruises leave from Pier 3. Scenic views can be enjoyed at piers 7 and 14. On the south waterfront, you'll find the 60-ft- (18-m-) tall Cupid's Span. It is a simple sculpture of the god's bow and arrow, which is half buried in the ground. It perfectly represents the city's romantic reputation. Piers north of the Ferry Building have odd numbers, while those to the south have even numbers.

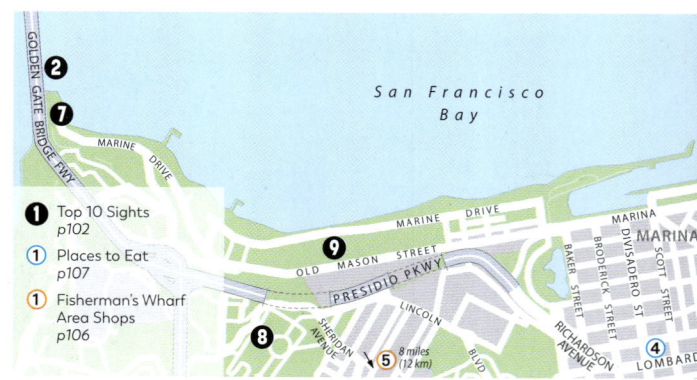

1 Top 10 Sights
p102

1 Places to Eat
p107

1 Fisherman's Wharf Area Shops
p106

For places to stay in this area, see p149

The gorgeous Golden Gate Bridge

2 Golden Gate Bridge

This renowned masterpiece of engineering *(p22)* sets off the entrance to San Francisco Bay in a spectacular way. It never fails to awe both first-timers and old-timers alike. Walking or cycling across its length is an unforgettable experience.

3 Angel and Treasure Islands

A trip out to Angel Island, now a state park, can mean a day of picnicking, biking, hiking, kayaking, swimming, or visiting the Immigration Museum and Barracks. But in the early 1900s it was the "Ellis Island of the West," where would-be immigrants, mostly Chinese, could be detained for months on end. During World War II, it served as a prisoner-of-war camp and then later as a missile base. Treasure Island was built in 1939 for the Golden Gate International Exposition and served as a US Navy base during World War II. It is now once again owned by the city of San Francisco.

4 Alcatraz Island

America's "Devil's Island" *(p28)* didn't operate as a prison for a particularly long time, but the cell blocks and control room still manage to evoke a chill.

5 Fisherman's Wharf

Although now largely tourist-oriented, there are still traditional maritime sights to see, aromas to savor, and salt air to breathe along these piers *(p26)*. PIER 39 is a highlight, with its various amusements, stores, and restaurants.

Whaleboat in the Maritime Museum, Aquatic Park

6 Aquatic Park
🚇 F1 🕐 10am–5pm daily
ℹ️ 499 Jefferson St; nps.gov/safr/learn/historyculture/aquatic-park-pier.htm

Within the sheltering arm of a curved fishing pier is the warmest, safest Bayside beach. Sometimes signs advise against swimming – look out before taking a dip in the cold water. Joggers and bikers love the paved trail. The cable car turn-around is steps away at Beach and Hyde streets. In the park, you will find a Visitor Center and the Maritime Museum *(p56)*.

7 Fort Point
🚇 C1

Crashing waves, passing ships, and windsurfers, along with a Civil War-era fort loaded with cannons, guns, and other military artifacts, make for spectacular photos here beneath the Golden Gate Bridge *(p22)*. You can fish along the seawall and take self-guided or ranger-led tours to learn about the building of the bridge. At the foot of the cliffs on the western side of the fort is a small beach loved by nude sun worshippers.

8 The Presidio
🚇 D2

This wooded corner of the city has stunning views over the Golden Gate. From 1776 until 1994, it was occupied by first the Spanish, then the Mexican, and finally, the US armies. It is now a major part of the Golden Gate National Recreational Area. It is full of nature trails, streams, forests, drives, and historic structures. Also here is the Walt Disney Family Museum, which gives insight into Walt Disney's life through photographs, animation, and a range of interactive exhibits.

9 Crissy Field
🚇 D1

Originally marshland and dunes, the field was filled in before the 1915 Panama-Pacific Exposition and then paved over for use as an airfield by the army from 1919 to 1936. With the esta-blishment of the Presidio as a National Park under the supervision of the city, a massive restoration project has returned part of Crissy Field to wetlands and the rest to lawns, pathways, and picnic areas. The city's over 4 million-sq-ft (370,000-sq-m) "Front Yard" is one of the prime view-ing sites for the Fourth of July fireworks. Extending over 4 miles (7 km), the Golden Gate Promenade is a paved

Historic Crissy Field with the San Francisco skyline in the backdrop

pathway that runs through this district from Aquatic Park to Fort Point.

10 Fort Mason Center

☑ F1

Since 1976, some of the buildings at this Civil War-era military base have been devoted to cultural programs. Some 50 cultural organizations now call it home. Among the most prominent are the Museo Italo Americano (p58), the Long Now Foundation, the Children's Art Center, and the Magic Theatre. One of the city's finest vegetarian restaurants, Greens, is also here, offering great views of the Bay (p107).

EARTHQUAKE! THE LANDFILL PROBLEM

Most of the Marina area and the Financial District was built on landfill. As time has proven, this was not such a good idea in a seismically active zone. When the Loma Prieta earthquake struck at 5:04pm on October 17, 1989, all such landfills liquefied, gas mains fractured, and several Marina homes slid off their foundations.

A BIKE RIDE THROUGH THE PRESIDIO

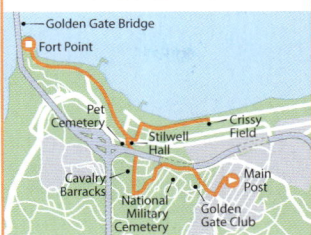

Beginning at the Visitor Information Center, where you can pick up an excellent map, first explore the **Main Post**. Here you can ride around the Parade Ground and see the earliest surviving buildings of the Presidio, dating from the 1860s, as well as 18th-century Spanish adobe wall fragments in the former Officers' Club.

Exit the area on Sheridan Avenue, which takes you past the **Golden Gate Club**, and turn left onto Lincoln Boulevard, which winds its way around the **National Military Cemetery**. Turn right on McDowell Avenue; on the left you will see the Colonial Revival **Cavalry Barracks**.

Now go past the five brick Stables, off to both the left and the right, and stop at the quirky **Pet Cemetery** on the left, where guard dogs are buried. Next, head under Highway 101 to encounter **Stilwell Hall**, built in 1921 as enlisted barracks and a mess hall for the airmen. Turn left to take in the metal **Aerodrome Hangars** from the same era, then proceed on and pause at **Crissy Field** to admire the views.

Double back at this point to take the next left down toward the Bay itself and join the Golden Gate Promenade all the way out to **Fort Point**. As long as the fog is not too bad, this is the perfect spot to experience the awe-inspiring **Golden Gate Bridge** (p22).

Fisherman's Wharf Area Shops

Tasty treats on display at the Ghirardelli Chocolate store

1. Ghirardelli Chocolate
K2 🏠 Ghirardelli Square, 900 North Point St 🌐 ghirardelli.com

Stop by for a free sample and then stock up on your mouth-watering favorites. Take home some chocolate cable cars.

2. Gigi + Rosie
K2 🏠 Ghirardelli Square, 900 North Point St 🌐 delilahstudios.com/gigiplusrosie

Quirky gifts, accessories, and children's outfits, many of which are designed by the owners, are for sale here.

3. Alcatraz Gift Shop
J4 🏠 2nd level, PIER 39 🌐 alcatrazgifts.com

Souvenirs of the Rock, from tin cups to prisoner outfits, are for sale here. Photos and history books can be found at the Alcatraz Book Store on Pier 41.

4. Real Old Paper
F1 🏠 777 Beach St 🌐 realoldpaper.com

Discover a beautiful selection of vintage posters from the US and elsewhere here.

5. Tunnel Records
F1 🏠 900 North Point E206 🌐 tunnelrecordssf.com

This local record shop specializes in jazz, soul, and rock vinyls.

6. V Boutique
F1 🏠 435 Jefferson St 📞 (415) 757-0043

This boutique selling stylish clothing for women is part of VenturaVie, a nonprofit funding local charity organizations and supporting local causes.

7. Patagonia
J4 🏠 770 North Point St 🌐 patagonia.com

The San Francisco store of this quintessentially Californian company sells classic fleeces and outdoor wear. One percent of annual sales is donated to environmental charities.

8. Alioto-Lazio Fish Co
F1 🏠 440 Jefferson St 🌐 crabonline.com

One of the last family-owned and operated fishing companies in San Francisco, Alioto-Lazio connects you to San Francisco's briny and delicious culinary heritage.

9. vomFASS
F1 🏠 900 North Point St 🌐 vomfassghirardellisquare.com

A locally owned store that sells organic wine, spirits, oil, and vinegar.

10. Frank's Fisherman
E1 🏠 366 Jefferson St 🌐 franksfishermansf.com

Frank's has been selling ship models, rare navigation devices, paintings, marine antiques, and various historic ship paraphernalia since 1946.

Places to Eat

1. Gary Danko

K2 **800 North Point St at Hyde** **garydanko.com · $$$**

The French American menu served here allows you to create your own fixed-price selection. If you don't have a reservation (which are taken up to two months in advance), head for the bar, where you can order anything on the menu.

2. The Codmother

J4 **496 Beach St** **D** **codmother.com · $**

This food truck serves outstanding fish tacos, fish and chips, and assorted chip-shop desserts, such as fried Oreos.

3. Isa

E2 **3324 Steiner St between Chestnut & Lombard** **L** **isarestaurant.com · $$**

At this tiny Marina restaurant, the concept is Nouvelle French tapas, with small plates such as honey-spiced calamari and lobster broth.

4. A16

E1 **2355 Chestnut St** **a16pizza.com · $$**

A traditional southern Italian dining experience that's worth getting dressed up for.

5. Tacolicious

K4 **2250 Chestnut St** **tacolicious.com · $**

A multitude of taco options are served at this popular joint. Enjoy the free chips and salsa while you wait.

6. Greens

F1 **Fort Mason Center, 2 Marina Blvd, Building A** **greensrestaurant. com · $$**

Since 1979, the inventive vegetarian dishes and Bayside panoramas here have delighted patrons.

7. Frascati

L2 **1901 Hyde St** **frascatisf.com · $$**

In a cozy atmosphere, Frascati offers Mediterranean cuisine with a Californian twist.

8. Scoma's

J2 **1965 Al Scoma Way** **scomas.com · $$**

A Fisherman's Wharf seafood tradition since 1965, Scoma's is well known for its cracked crab roasted in garlic.

9. Zushi Puzzle

F2 **1910 Lombard St** **L** **zushipuzzle.com · $$**

This spot serves some of the city's best sushi.

10. The Buena Vista Café

K2 **2765 Hyde St** **thebuenavista.com · $**

This café claims to have invented Irish coffee. The menu features classic American dishes.

Bartender mixing Irish coffees at The Buena Vista Café

CENTRAL NEIGHBORHOODS

As is the case with most parts of San Francisco, diversity is the keynote here. These areas encompass the oldest money and the highest society of the founding families of the city, as well as some of its most disadvantaged communities. Here you can trace the evolution of San Francisco, from the sophisticated old streets of Pacific Heights and Presidio Heights, via the hippie-era Flower Power of Haight-Ashbury, to the redeveloped neighborhoods such as Hayes Valley, buzzing with boutiques and trendy spots to eat and drink. Some of the city's most iconic sights are found in these central neighborhoods, from the colorful Victorian row homes to the counterculture hangouts lining Golden Gate Park.

For places to stay in this area, see p149

1 Golden Gate Park

One of the largest public parks in the world *(p36)* complete with cultural attractions including the California Academy of Sciences and the de Young Museum.

2 Pacific Heights

Q E2

A grander, more exclusive residential area is hard to imagine. The blocks between Alta Plaza and Lafayette parks are the very heart of the area, but the grandeur extends from Gough Street to Divisadero Street and beyond. On a sunny day, there's nothing more exhilarating than scaling its hills and taking in the perfectly manicured streets, the views, and the palatial dwellings. The Spreckels Mansion, a limestone palace in the Beaux Arts tradition, on Washington and Octavia streets, is the brightest gem of the lot, now owned by the novelist Danielle Steel.

3 Union Street

Q E2

A neighborhood shopping artery loaded with tradition, Union Street is noted for its sidewalk cafés, bookstores, and designer boutiques, all housed in converted Victorian charmers. The street is at the heart of the Cow Hollow neighborhood, whose name recalls its previous life as a dairy pasture.

Cable cars and pedestrians on Union Street

4 Japantown

Q F3

This neighborhood has been the center of the city's Japanese community since the early 20th century. The Japan Center was built as part of an ambitious 1960s post-World War II Japanese American incarceration plan to revitalize the Fillmore District. Blocks of aging Victorian buildings were demolished and replaced by the Geary Expressway and this Japanese-style shopping complex with a five-tiered, 75-ft (22-m) Peace Pagoda at its heart. Taiko drummers perform here during the Cherry Blossom Festival each April *(p88)*. The extensive malls are lined with traditional Japanese shops and restaurants, an eight-screen movie theater, and the Kabuki Springs and Spa. More stores and restaurants can be found along the outdoor mall across Post Street.

5 The Richmond District

Q C3

This flat district of row houses begins at Masonic Avenue, sandwiched between Golden Gate Park and California Street. It ultimately extends all the way to the Pacific Ocean, being more and more prone to stay fogbound the farther west you go. The district is very multicultural and generally middle class. Over the decades, it has been settled by Russians, East European Jews, and latterly Chinese Americans and another wave of Russians.

6 Presidio Heights
🅿 D3

Originally part of the "Great Sand Waste" to the west, this neighborhood is now one of the most elite of all. The zone centers on Sacramento Street as its discreet shopping area. It's worth a stroll, primarily for the architecture. Of interest are the Swedenborgian Church at 2107 Lyon Street, the Roos House at 3500 Jackson Street, and Temple Emanu-El at 2 Lake Street.

7 Geary Boulevard
🅿 F3

One of the city's main traffic arteries, sweeping from Van Ness all the way out to Cliff House, Geary Boulevard is a typically unprepossessing and functional urban thoroughfare. It begins its journey at Market Street, sweeping past Union Square, and then forms the heart of the Theater District, before venturing into the notorious Tenderloin District. After it crosses Van Ness, it zips past Japantown and the funky Fillmore District. Soon you're in the Richmond District and before you know it, there's the Pacific Ocean.

8 Hayes Valley
🅿 F4

This small area has seen a massive change over the past few decades. Once a run-down neighborhood, Hayes Valley is now synonymous

with great boutique shopping and popular cafés. The dismantling of an unsightly freeway overpass following the 1989 earthquake helped turn the tide, and the welcome result is a chic area that hasn't lost its edge. Hayes Valley festivals take place in mid-summer, when the area's streets are thronged with revelers.

9 Western Addition
🅿 E3

This area, once sandy waste, was transformed after World War II when African Americans from the South moved west in search of work during the Great Migration. In the 1940s and 1950s, the Fillmore District here became known as the "Harlem of the West," famous for its jazz and blues clubs later embodied by John Lee Hooker and his Boom Boom Room, until his death in 2001. Today, the area is best known for getting a snapshot of local life, plus seeing the architecturally odd Cathedral of St. Mary of the Assumption (p55) and photogenic Alamo Square (p55).

Geometric design of the Cathedral of St. Mary of the Assumption

Pastel-colored homes, nicknamed
the Painted Ladies, Haight-Ashbury

10 Haight-Ashbury
□ D4

This anarchic quarter is one of the
most scintillating and unconventional
in the city, resting firmly on its laurels
as ground zero for the worldwide Flower
Power explosion of the 1960s (p53).
Admire the beautiful old Queen Anne-
style houses, a few of them still painted
in the psychedelic pigments of the
hippie era, as well as the unique stores
and the venerable Haight-Ashbury
Food Program. The Lower Haight is
noted for its edgy clubs and bars.

FLOWER POWER

In 1967, San Francisco witnessed the
Summer of Love (p53), including the
75,000-strong Human Be-In at Golden
Gate Park. People were drawn here –
many with flowers in their hair – by
the acid-driven melodies of Jefferson
Airplane, Janis Joplin, Jimi Hendrix,
and The Doors. Soon, however, public
alarm, and too many bad acid trips,
caused the bubble to burst.

A TOUR OF HAIGHT-ASHBURY

Begin at **Alamo Square** (p55), with
the Westerfeld House at 1198 Fulton
at Scott, former residence of Ken
Kesey, the writer and visionary
who arguably got the whole
1960s movement going. Walk up
Scott, turn right on Page and go
to No. 1090, where the rock band
Big Brother and the Holding
Company got their start. A block
and a half farther on, go right
on Lyon to No. 122, where Janis
Joplin (p61) lived for most of 1967.

Continue on to the **Panhandle**
(Stanyan St & Fell St), an extension
of Golden Gate Park, where, in June
1967, The Jimi Hendrix Experience
gave a free concert. Now turn left
on Central and head up to steep
Buena Vista Park (Buena Vista &
Haight St), site of public Love-Ins
in the 1960s and 1970s. Turn right
on Haight and check out **Love On
Haight** (loveonhaightsf.com), a tie-
dye emporium dedicated to keeping
the Summer of Love spirit alive.

Continue on to the Haight-Ashbury
intersection and walk along Haight
to Clayton; at No. 558 is the much-
loved **Haight-Ashbury Free Clinic**.
Later, stop in for a snack at
Blue Front Café.

Refreshed, walk toward Golden
Gate Park, then turn right on
Stanyan all the way to Fulton. At
2400 Fulton stands the former
Jefferson Airplane Mansion.
Finally, head into **Golden Gate
Park** (p36) and make your way
to the drum circles on Hippie
Hill to groove to the funky beats.

Shops

**Handmade toy zebra
for sale at Sue Fisher King**

1. The Love of Ganesha
📍E4 🏠1573 Haight St 📞(415) 863-0999

More than just a clothing store, this unique boutique features a selection of crystals, stones, and other natural knickknacks that you can't find anywhere else in the city.

2. Daiso Japan
📍F3 🏠22 Peace Plaza 🖥daisos.com

Discount store selling Japanese household items, snacks, and other fun imports.

3. Dark Garden
📍F4 🏠321 Linden St
🖥darkgarden.com

Popular shop for women's couture and locally made, custom and ready-to-wear corsets, dresses, and wedding gowns.

4. Dottie Doolittle
📍D3 🏠3680 Sacramento St
🖥dottiedoolittle.com

A long-established mainstay, this high-end clothier carries fashionable American and European labels for babies and kids up to the age of 12.

5. Past Perfect
📍B3 🏠6101 Geary Blvd
🖥pastperfectsf.com

There is tons to choose from at this huge, fairly priced vintage store. Plan to spend a while perusing their unique furniture, lighting, and art – there is something for everyone here. The staff are friendly, too.

6. Forest Books
📍F3 🏠1748 Buchanan St
📞(415) 563-8302

Specializing in secondhand, rare, and collectible books, this inviting, family-run bookstore sells excellent titles across fiction, philosophy, Eastern religions, and spirituality.

7. Sue Fisher King
📍F2 🏠1913 Fillmore 🖥suefisherking.com

In 1978, Sue Fisher King opened her shop of trinkets and treasures for the home, fine jewelry, and divinely scented bath products. Today, it's still considered one of the city's must-visits.

8. Isotope – The Comic Book Lounge
📍F4 🏠326 Fell St 📞(415) 621-6543

With plenty of space for customers to browse and sit, Isotope offers comics, graphic novels, and handmade zines. Local artists are often invited to give talks and hold book signings, and the owner is happy to help shoppers.

9. Relic Vintage
📍E4 🏠1475 Haight St
🖥relicvintagesf.com

The city's most carefully curated vintage clothing, from suits to swing coats, can be found at this welcoming Haight Street shop. Owner Oran Scott is always dressed to the nines.

10. Amoeba Music
📍D4 🏠1855 Haight St 🖥amoeba.com

Besides thousands of LPs, tapes, and CDs, there's also a huge selection of DVDs and posters at this record store, a perennial local favorite, and it prides itself on being the world's largest independent music store.

Places to Eat

1. Perry's
F2 **1944 Union St**
perryssf.com · $
A San Francisco institution, noted for its burgers and other all-American favorites, including meatloaf, prime rib, and fried chicken.

2. State Bird Provisions
F3 **1529 Fillmore St**
statebirdsf.com · $$$
A trendy Michelin-starred restaurant serving small plates of French and American fare. Choose most of your food from a cart or tray of dishes brought out by the waiting staff.

3. SPQR
E3 **1911 Fillmore St**
spqrsf.com · $$$
Reservations are required at this Michelin-starred, rustic, Roman-inspired restaurant, with superior service and mouthwatering dishes that mix Italian and Californian elements.

4. Nopa
E4 **560 Divisadero St**
L **nopasf.com · $$**
Considered one of the best restaurants in the city, Nopa's menu changes with the seasons.

5. Absinthe
F4 **398 Hayes St** **Mon & Tue**
absinthe.com · $$
This Parisian-style bistro serves specials such as the extremely popular *foie gras torchon*.

6. Pizzeria Delfina
F5 **2406 California St**
pizzeriadelfina.com · $
Rustic, simple, and fresh, this popular farm-to-table pizzeria serves incredible Neapolitan thin-crust pizzas in addition to delicious, traditional antipasti, salami, beer, wine, and more.

7. Spruce
D3 **3640 Sacramento St**
sprucesf.com · $$$
One of the best restaurants in the city, Spruce has a meat-heavy menu.

8. Udon Mugizo
F3 **Japantown Center, 1581 Webster St** **mugizo-us.com · $**
A cozy spot in Japantown serving a variety of excellent noodles.

9. Daeho
F3 **1620 Post St** **daeho-kalbijjim.com · $**
One of San Francisco's best Korean restaurants, Daeho specializes in *kalbijjim*, a delicious short-rib stew.

10. Arizmendi
F5 **1286 Valencia St**
arizmendibakery.com · $
This delightful cooperative serves artisan breads and a range of pizzas.

Bartender preparing Spanish coffee at Absinthe

SOUTHERN NEIGHBORHOODS

The southern part of San Francisco comprises some of the liveliest and most diverse parts of the city, including the clubs of SoMa, the LGBTQ+ world of the Castro, and the Latin American Mission District. With high rents and real estate prices forcing lower-income residents out of the city center and into the south, many of the neighborhoods on this side of the city have become popular with locals seeking more affordable housing. Noe Valley was the first such choice, but gentrification there has pushed people farther south to up-and-coming areas such as Bernal Heights and Glen Park.

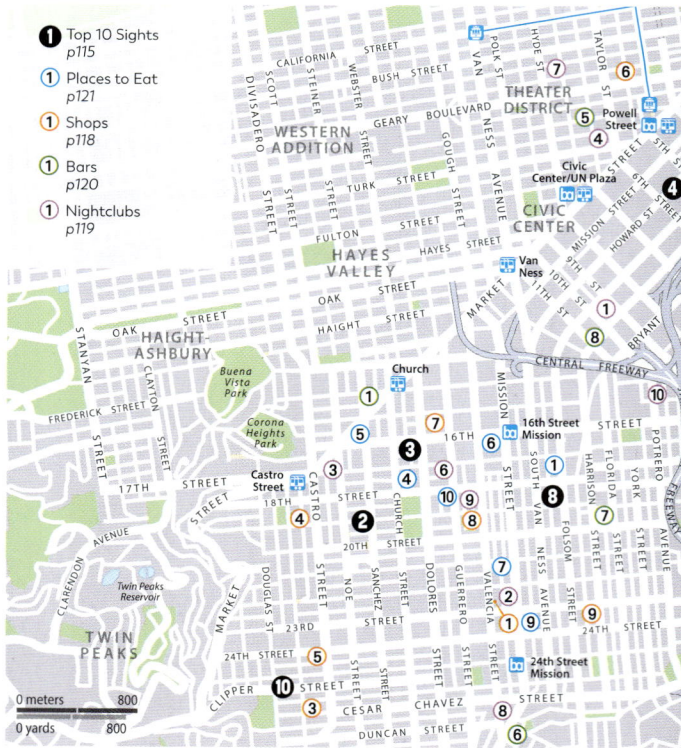

Top 10 Sights
p115

Places to Eat
p121

Shops
p118

Bars
p120

Nightclubs
p119

For places to stay in this area, see p150

1 South Beach and Mission Bay
📍 H4

This old shipping port area was revitalized with the addition of Oracle Park, a venue for numerous concerts throughout the year, and home to the San Francisco Giants – the city's Major League Baseball team. Many restaurants and sports bars have opened up here. There are several entertainment options, including a bowling alley, which attract families and sports fans alike to this waterfront neighborhood.

2 Castro District
📍 E5

This neighborhood, with the historic Castro Theatre, is the center of the city's LGBTQ+ community. The intersection

Rainbow crosswalk in the Castro District

of Castro and 18th streets is known as the "Gayest Four Corners of the World." This district emerged in the 1970s as a pilgrimage for gay travelers from all over the world. The lively Castro Street Fair (castrostreetfair.org) is held here every year.

3 Mission Dolores
📍 F5 🏛 3321 16th St at Dolores St
🕐 10am–4pm Tue–Sun 🌐 mission dolores.org

The Spanish Misión San Francisco de Asís, from which the city takes its name, is a marvel of preservation and atmospheric charm. It was founded in 1776, a few weeks before the Declaration of Independence.

4 South of Market (SoMa)
📍 R4

This former rough-and-tumble warehouse district now houses the SFMOMA and SoMa Pilipinas Cultural Heritage District. Some of the city's best eating joints, bars, and galleries are in SoMa.

5 Yerba Buena Gardens
📍 R4 🕐 6am–10pm daily
🌐 yerbabuenagardens.org

Teeming with art installations, green spaces, and museums, all spread out across several modern buildings, the Yerba Buena Gardens (p44) feel like a mini artists' community.

6 Potrero Hill
H5

This SoMa hill was once set to become the next big thing, but its isolation kept that from happening, cut off from the rest of the city, as it is, by freeways on three sides and its own precipitous inclines. It has remained a quiet neighborhood with spectacular views. There are restaurants, bars, and many design stores here. Notable spots for live music include Thee Parkside (thee parkside.com) and Bottom of the Hill (p120).

7 San Francisco Museum of Modern Art (SFMOMA)

San Francisco's home for its extensive modern art collection (p42) is as impressive outside as it is awe-inspiring inside. Its expansive galleries allow a great amount of its stunning treasure of paintings, photography, media and digital installations, designs, and sculptures to be on show.

8 Mission District
F5

The Mission District is home to much of the city's Latin American community. Its streets are lined with Mexican taquerias, Salvadoran restaurants, and other Latino-owned businesses, alongside trendy boutiques and vintage shops. This historic neighborhood also has a lively nightlife, with arguably the city's best club and bar scene. The two-day free Carnaval (p88) celebration, held annually in late spring, is not to be missed.

9 Moscone Center
Q5 **Howard St**

Embellishing the SoMa cultural and business district, the Moscone Center consists of an impressive central building, as well as a new, glass-enclosed expansion. The city's largest convention space also features an arrival plaza, enclosed bridges, and gardens, all connecting the

Distinctive red-brick facade of the SFMOMA

Inside the impressive
Moscone Center

massive three-block facility to surrounding hotels, theaters, restaurants, museums, and parks.

10 Noe Valley

☑ E6

Once a simple working-class neighborhood, Noe Valley saw an influx of hippies, the LGBTQ+ community, and artists in the 1970s, which made it an attractive alternative to more established quarters. In its hey-day, it was known as both "Nowhere Valley" for its relative remoteness and "Granola Valley" for its nature-loving denizens. Lately, it has been taken over by middle-class professionals, who value it for its orderliness, but 24th Street still hums with activity and is lined with cafés and bookstores.

A WALK AROUND THE CASTRO DISTRICT

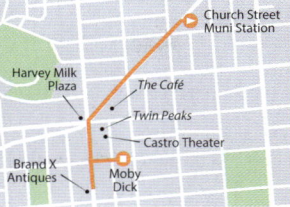

Begin at the LGBTQ+ hub of San Francisco, the **Church Street Muni Station** on Upper Market. Decades ago, this corner became the symbolic starting point of the Castro neighborhood, but it is on the next block, between Sanchez and Noe, that the LGBTQ+ shops and venues really proliferate. Toward the corner of Castro is the popular nightclub **The Café** (p119), offering a range of strong drinks.

Continuing on to Castro Street, take in **Harvey Milk Plaza**, with its huge rainbow flag; the plaza is named for the first openly gay politician elected to public office in California, who was assassinated in 1978. On the opposite corner, check out **Twin Peaks** (p79), the first gay bar in the country, notable for its street-facing windows, which allow passersby to see inside.

Pushing on to No. 429, allow the **Castro Theatre** to capture your attention. One of the city's most ornate cinema palaces, it hosts a number of premieres of films with LGBTQ+ themes. Farther along at No. 570, **Brand X Antiques** (p118) is a great place to browse, with its eclectic collection of goods, ranging from furniture to homoerotica. On Hartford Street, **Moby Dick** (p78) is a popular spot that attracts a steady crowd of regulars. Finish here to shoot some pool or pinball while enjoying 1980s tunes with a well-earned drink.

Shops

1. Needles and Pens
 F5 1173 Valencia St
 needles-pens.com
There's a little bit of everything at this funky, eclectic store. Don't miss the fantastic magazine selection, unique cards, stationery, and T-shirts, as well as the gallery.

2. WearSomethingRare
 R6 440 Brannan St
 (415) 795-4105
Limited production clothing made on-site by local, talented designers. Watch your shirt being sewed in the factory at the back.

3. Omnivore Books on Food
 F6 3885 Cesar Chavez St
 omnivorebooks.myshopify.com
Located in the Mission District, this bookstore specializes in food-related titles. Pick up the latest foodie memoirs, discover new cookbooks, or attend events featuring celebrity chefs here.

4. Brand X Antiques
 E5 570 Castro St
 (415) 626-8908
The gay couple who own this shop share a discerning and humorous eye for antiques. In addition to baubles, rings, and furniture, the collection also features tongue-in-cheek vintage homoerotica.

5. Wink San Francisco
 E5 4107 24th St winksf.com
A large gift shop brimming with personality, thanks to a whimsical selection of eccentric books, toys, and home decor.

6. City Art Gallery
 F5 828 Valencia St between 19th & 20th Noon–9pm Wed–Sun
 cityartgallery.org
This gallery sells reasonably priced works of art, making it a great spot to find a unique gift.

7. Creativity Explored
 F4 3245 16th St
 creativityexplored.org
Celebrating artists with developmental disabilities, this studio and gallery space has an amazing store selling the artists' works, from prints and sculptures to t-shirts and pins.

8. Wilkes Bashford
 P4 375 Sutter St
 wilkesbashford.com
Founded in 1966, Wilkes Bashford is a family-owned luxury clothing store that styles San Francisco's elite. Wilkes Bashford stocks high-end designs, including fine footwear. The on-site tailor customizes any purchases as desired.

9. Medicine for Nightmares
 G5 3036 24th St medicinefornightmares.com
This bookstore offers a wide range of titles, including children's books, and regularly hosts events such as author talks, spoken-word poetry nights, and art exhibitions.

10. Paxton Gate
 F5 824 Valencia St
 paxtongate.com
This wonderland of unique gifts and home decor even includes strange pieces of taxidermy. Kids will love this place as much as adults.

Arranging the books at Omnivore Books on Food

Nightclubs

1. Powerhouse
📍 G4 🏠 1347 Folsom St 🕐 Tue
🌐 powerhousebar.com

One of the city's most popular, anything-goes gay leather bar Powerhouse is a welcoming and safe space. The basic decor complements the no-frills stiff drinks.

2. Make-Out Room
📍 F5 🏠 3225 22nd St at Mission 🌐 makeoutroom.com

Live music and DJ nights make this cool club a Mission favorite. The decor is unique and the drinks are reasonably priced.

3. The Café
📍 E5 🏠 2369 Market St at Castro 🌐 thecafesf.com

There is something (and someone) for everybody at this camp, cruisy, Castro old-timer that welcomes all. The outdoor balcony is great for people-watching.

4. Aunt Charlie's Lounge
📍 Q3 🏠 133 Turk St 🌐 auntcharlies lounge.com

This legendary drag bar, an icon of San Francisco's nightlife, is known for its dive-bar vibe, affordable drinks, and lively dance floor.

5. The EndUp
📍 R4 🏠 401 6th St at Harrison 🌐 theendupsf.com

Formerly exclusively gay, as famously featured in the novel series *Tales of the City* by Armistead Maupin, this classic bar is now thoroughly mixed, featuring house music, and is one of the city's best after-hours clubs.

6. 500 Club
📍 F4 🏠 500 Guerrero St
📞 (415) 861-2500

Cheap, stiff drinks, loud music, and plenty of seating space make

Bright neon sign above the entrance of 500 Club

this place a trendy, local favorite. You cannot miss the neon sign that points to the entrance.

7. The Royale
📍 G2 🏠 800 Post St 🌐 theroyalesf.com

This thriving club hosts everything from art exhibits to live jazz concerts. The bar offers a huge selection of wines and beers.

8. El Rio
📍 F5 🏠 3158 Mission St 🌐 elriosf.com

Different dance and live-music events organized every night of the week draw a diverse crowd ready to do their thing at this bar, which opened in 1978. Sunday Salsa Showcase is particularly popular.

9. The Chapel
📍 F5 🏠 777 Valencia St
🌐 thechapelsf.com

Formerly a chapel, this place now showcases live music and comedy acts by local as well as national artists. Have dinner or drinks prior to the performance at the attached cocktail bar, Curio.

10. The Great Northern
📍 G4 🏠 119 Utah St at 15th
🌐 thegreatnorthernsf.com

Popular hip-hop and house DJs keep the crowds dancing at this large nightclub, which doubles as an art gallery.

Well-stocked bar at the Hotel Utah Saloon

Bars

1. Café du Nord
📍 F4 🏠 2174 Market St
🌐 cafedunord.com

Located in the landmark Swedish American Hall, this music venue, restaurant, and cocktail bar is one of the smartest the city has to offer.

2. Bottom of the Hill
📍 G4 🏠 1233 17th St between Texas & Missouri 🌐 bottomofthehill.com

This legendary live-music venue features punk, rock, and folk bands, and has a pleasant back patio for beer breaks.

3. Moshi Moshi
📍 H5 🏠 2092 3rd St
🌐 moshimoshisf.com

This Californian-Japanese restaurant has an impressive collection of Japanese whiskey. The owner is always happy to guide customers on what to order.

4. Rooftop 25
📍 H3 🏠 25 Lush St 🌐 25lush.com

Located in a timber warehouse, this rooftop bar is sleek and modern with a hip, urban vibe. The cocktails are delicious, and the stylish lounge below is great for people-watching.

5. Bourbon & Branch
📍 P3 🏠 501 Jones St 🌐 bourbonandbranch.com

This classy 1920s-style speakeasy serves creative cocktails. The secret rooms have a Prohibition-era atmosphere. Come here for hard-to-find liquors.

6. The Knockout
📍 F6 🏠 3223 Mission St
🌐 theknockoutsf.com

With DJs and live music all week, and bingo on Thursdays, The Knockout has remained one of the most popular dive bars in San Francisco for years.

7. Trick Dog
📍 F5 🏠 3010 20th St
🌐 trickdogbar.com

Well-crafted and imaginative cocktails win rave reviews at this split-level bar in the Mission District. It has innovative decor and delicious bar snacks.

8. DNA Lounge
📍 F4 🏠 375 11th St 🌐 dnalounge.com

A popular party spot, this nightclub and restaurant features live events such as electronic music, rock bands, and DJ sets. Enjoy local offbeat entertainment such as theater, burlesque, and spoken-word performances.

9. Hotel Utah Saloon
📍 R5 🏠 500 4th St 🌐 hotelutah.com

This Gold-Rush-themed bar, with a honky-tonk atmosphere, hosts live local music acts and has a long bar.

10. 21st Amendment
📍 R6 🏠 563 2nd St
🌐 21st-amendment.com

A sports fan's dream, this brewpub serves up handcrafted beers and standard American fare. It's a friendly place to catch a game on television.

Places to Eat

1. Stable Café
F5 2128 Folsom at 17th St
Mon stablecafe.com · $
Homemade breakfast and lunch options here center on freshly baked breads and healthy local ingredients.

2. Marlowe
H3 500 Brannan St
marlowesf.com · $$
This cozy yet chic restaurant serves outstanding bistro dishes.

3. Prospect
H2 300 Spear St
prospectsf.com · $$$
One of the city's most stand-out meals can be had at this SoMa mainstay.

4. Tartine Bakery and Café
F5 600 Guerrero St
tartinebakery.com · $
The award-winning breads, cakes, and pastries here draw a crowd. Be prepared to wait in line.

5. Kitchen Story
F4 3499 16th St
kitchenstorysf.com · $$$
This restaurant offers excellent Asian-inspired Californian brunch fare. Arrive hungry to enjoy hearty egg dishes, the famous Millionaire's Bacon, and award-winning Bloody Marys.

6. Pancho Villa Taqueria
F4 3071 16th St
sfpanchovilla.com · $
This is one of the best Mexican restaurants in the city, serving tacos and burritos at low prices.

7. Foreign Cinema
F5 2534 Mission St
foreigncinema.com · $$
Entertaining guests by screening old and new movies as they dine, Foreign Cinema is a recurring name on the *San Francisco Chronicle*'s list of the city's top 100 restaurants.

8. Sana'a Cafe
G3 199 New Montgomery St
sanaahousecafe.com · $$
The passion for Yemeni coffee at this café is evident in its specialty coffee drinks, infused with cardamom and cinnamon. Enjoy a cup alongside the delicious sweet and savory pastries.

9. El Farolito
F5 2779 Mission St at 24th
elfarolitosf.com · $
Line up for superb tacos, generous Mission-style burritos, and other hot dishes at this bright, buzzing place.

10. Delfina
F5 3621 18th St L
delfinasf.com · $$
Delfina serves perfect Italian fare. Its next-door pizzeria *(p113)* is ideal for a more casual dinner.

Neatly set tables at the Italian restaurant Delfina

OCEANFRONT

As with every part of the city, this area is a study in contrasts. It contains varied terrains of natural, untamed beauty – particularly the breathtaking, windswept cliffs and hidden ravines of Lands End, the scene of innumerable shipwrecks. Yet, just a few blocks away is Sea Cliff, one of the most exclusive and expensive residential neighborhoods in San Francisco, with its excellent ocean views. Of all the city's areas, this is where you're almost certain to encounter the infamous fog, but if the weather is clear, it's possible to spot the offshore Seal Rocks and even the fabled Farallon Islands.

1 Top 10 Sights
p123

1 Places to Eat
p127

1 Shops
p126

For places to stay in this area, see p150

Beachgoers enjoying a stroll on Ocean Beach

1 Ocean Beach
A4 🗺 The Great Hwy

Most of the western boundary of San Francisco is defined by this broad sweep of sand. Although it is a sublime sight when viewed from Cliff House or Sutro Heights Park, do note that it is dangerous to swim in the the ocean here due to icy waters, rough shore breakers, and, most of all, rip currents that are powerful enough to drag even strong swimmers out to sea. Nevertheless, hardy Californian surfers in thick wetsuits are a common sight here, and, in fine weather, sunbathers and picnickers materialize to loll on the sand and enjoy the sunshine.

2 Beach Chalet
A4 🗺 1000 Great Hwy
📞 (415) 386-8439

This 1925 colonial-revival style building was originally the Golden Gate Park Chalet, before becoming an Army headquarters, and then a dive bar. It's now a spectacular place to eat. On the first floor, the historic frescoes of life in San Francisco in the 1930s are a delight. Upstairs, the sweeping views of the beach and the crashing Pacific waves are enchanting, especially at sunset. The menu features an array of San Francisco staples like cioppino (fish stew) with ales and lagers that are crafted on site.

3 Legion of Honor
B3 🗺 100 34th Ave, Lincoln Park 🕐 9:30am–5:15pm Tue–Sun 🌐 famsf.org

The creation of Alma de Bretteville Spreckels, heiress to the Spreckels sugar fortune, this museum is a replica of the Palais de la Légion d'Honneur in Paris.

The original structure was built for the 1915 Panama-Pacific Exposition, but Mrs. Spreckels wanted to build a permanent version and employed the same architect she commissioned for her mansion in Pacific Heights (p109). It opened in 1924 and features medieval to 20th-century European art, with paintings by Monet and Rembrandt.

4 Oceanfront Parks
A3

Lincoln Park, Lands End, and Sutro Heights Park are large green areas overlooking the coast along this northwestern corner of the peninsula. Lincoln Park is the work of John McClaren (p37), and has trails with some of the best views of the Golden Gate Bridge. Lands End is a rugged stretch along the cliffs that features a picturesque cove and spectacular hiking. Statuary of the old Sutro estate still decorates Sutro Heights Park, which dominates the coastal scene from its vantage point.

5 Sigmund Stern Grove
🗺 Sloat Blvd at 19th Ave, Sunset 🌐 sterngrove.org

This 33-acre (13-ha) ravine in the southern Sunset District was donated to the city of San Francisco by Rosalie M. Stern in 1931, in memory of her husband Sigmund, a civic leader. It is the site of the nation's original free summer arts festival, Stern Grove Festival. Running on Sunday afternoons, the program may include classical music performed by the San Francisco Symphony Orchestra, opera, jazz, popular music, or productions by the San Francisco Ballet. The natural amphitheater has great acoustics.

6 Seal Rocks
🅟 A3

The westernmost promontory on this tip of the peninsula is Point Lobos, the projection that forms the rocky cove of Lands End. Along to the south from here down to Cliff House is a scattering of small, rocky islands that are frequented by seals. At night, from the beach or Cliff House promenade, the barking of the sea lions – like the keening of the foghorns – is both reassuring and eerie, and so very "San Francisco." On a clear day, 32 miles (50 km) off the coast, you can see the Farallon Islands, which are also inhabited by sea lions and have a state-protected rookery.

7 Sea Cliff
🅟 C2

Many famous residents, such as Twitter (now X) founder Jack Dorsey and actress Sharon Stone, have had homes in this elite residential enclave, which stands in stark contrast to the natural coastal area all around it. Most of the luxurious homes are Mediterranean in style and date from the 1920s. Just below the neighborhood, China Beach *(p66)*, which was named after Chinese fishers who used to camp here, is one of the safest beaches in the city for swimming and is equipped with showers. Baker Beach *(p66)*, just to the north, is another popular beach.

8 Lake Merced
🅟 Hwy 35

Located at the beginning of scenic Skyline Boulevard (Hwy 35), this lake, set amid verdant hills, extends across the southern end of the Sunset District. Relatively undeveloped and underused, it nevertheless gets its share of recreation enthusiasts. They come for the municipal 18-hole TPC Harding Park golf course, as well as the biking and running trails that circle the lake's green shoreline.

9 San Francisco Zoo
🅟 Sloat Blvd at the Great Hwy 🕙 Summer: 10am–5pm daily (last entry 4pm); winter: 9:30am–4:30pm daily (last entry 3:30pm) 🌐 sfzoo.org 🔶

San Francisco Zoo is at the far southwest corner of the city,

**Seal Rocks, a haven
for sea lions**

between the Pacific Ocean and Lake
Merced. The complex is home to more
than 1,000 species. Gorilla Preserve,
Grizzly Gulch, Koala Crossing, and
Children's Zoo are particular hits, as are
the feeding times for the grizzly bears
and the penguins. Summer brings a
busy program of extra activities
in the Children's Zoo.

10 Sunset District

🄩 C5 🄰 West-central
**San Francisco, between Sloat
Blvd & Golden Gate Park**

Like its counterpart the Richmond
District *(p109)*, this neighborhood
was originally part of the Outer
Lands, areas once thought to be
uninhabitable. Today, it is mostly
residential, consisting of row upon row
of neat, lookalike houses. Notable
highlights here include the distinctive
three-legged Sutro Tower, standing
977-ft (298-m) tall, and a variety of
high-quality family-owned restaurants,
with a special focus on Chinese cuisine.
However, like much of the area along
the ocean, this district is subject to
a great deal of gray weather.

**Sutro Tower standing
tall above the city**

A TWO-HOUR HIKE
AROUND LANDS END

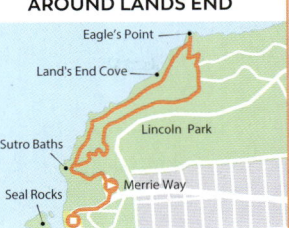

This section of the coast is
amazingly wild. Note that portions
of the hike are very rugged, so dress
accordingly, with sturdy footwear.

Begin at the far end of the Merrie
Way parking lot and take the steps
down. Follow the trail that passes
by the Sutro Baths ruins, to your
left as you descend. Continue
along to the Overlook, from where
you can take in **Seal Rocks** and
much of the Pacific panorama.

Now double back a bit to pick up
the trail that continues along the
coast. You will see the remains of
concrete military bunkers, which
have been broken and tilted by
the unstable land. Soon you will
come to a beach below rocky
cliffs; note that the surging water
is very unpredictable here, so be
very careful. Continue walking
and you will arrive at Lands End
Cove, where a makeshift beach,
using rock walls as windbreakers,
is popular with nudists.

Next, climb up the wooden steps
to join the path above and continue on around the bend, where
a stunning view of the **Golden
Gate Bridge** *(p22)* will greet you.
Continue walking all the way to
Eagle's Point and then return by
way of the higher trail that winds
through **Lincoln Park**.

If you have worked up an
appetite from your hike, enjoy
a meal and the wonderful views
at **The Art Bistro** *(415-379-7119)*,
located nearby.

Shops

Kura Revolving Sushi Bar in Stonestown Galleria

1. Park Life
📍 D3 🏠 220 Clement St
🌐 parklifestore.com

Part retail store, part art gallery, this sleek space features limited-edition books, prints, homeware, jewelry, T-shirts, and art. The gallery also exhibits contemporary art.

2. The Last Straw
📍 A5 🏠 4540 Irving St
🌐 laststrawsf.com

This tiny store near the beach has been run by the same friendly owner for more than 30 years. Great, interesting pieces of jewelry and unique finds are on sale here.

3. Gaslight and Shadows Antiques
📍 C3 🏠 2335 Clement St
🌐 gaslightshadows.com

The specialty here is porcelain, specifically the delicate master-pieces turned out by various makers in the town of Limoges, France. It's like visiting a museum dedicated to this fine art form.

4. Paul's Hat Works
📍 B3 🏠 6128 Geary Blvd
🌐 hatworksbypaul.com

This one-of-a-kind store is devoted to old-fashioned hat-making. Each hat is custom-made by appointment, though same-day walk-ins are always welcome.

5. Aqua Surf Shop
📍 A5 🏠 3847 Judah St
🌐 aquasurfshop.com

Find every sort of surf gear here, including the extra-thick wetsuits needed to survive these northern waters.

6. Stonestown Galleria
🏠 3251 20th Ave at Winston Drive
🌐 stonestowngalleria.com

This mall offers a mix of local and national vendors, including Matcha Cafe Maiko, Marugame Udon, and the charming Miniso. There's also a Regal Cinema and YMCA.

7. Green Apple Books
📍 D3 🏠 506 Clement St
🌐 greenapplebooks.com

It's easy to lose a few hours browsing through the selection of used books and DVDs at this store. Part of the fun in taking the time to read the well-written and helpful staff recommendations.

8. Foggy Notion
📍 D3 🏠 124 Clement St
🌐 foggy-notion.com

An eco-conscious boutique store that specializes in handmade home and health products, ranging from body oils to scented candles inspired by the coast of California.

9. Kamei Housewares
📍 D3 🏠 547 Clement St
📞 (415) 666-3688

This large store has essential equipment for cooking Asian cuisines, and a wonderful selection of tableware and tea sets.

10. See's Candies
🏠 3251 20th Ave, Stonestown Galleria
🌐 chocolateshops.sees.com

Founded in 1921 by Charles See, this traditional shop offers high-quality chocolates, truffles, brittles, toffees, and lollipops.

Places to Eat

1. TJ Café
A4 🏠 724 La Playa St
W tjcafesf.com · $
This café serves simple but delicious American bites, as well as fish and chips, which you can easily take with you to enjoy at the nearby Ocean Beach.

2. Beach Chalet Brewery
A4 🏠 1000 Great Hwy
W beachchalet.com · $$
People come to this charming venue for the views – both of the ocean and the murals – as well as for the food.

3. Kabuto Sushi
C3 🏠 5121 Geary Blvd at 15th Ave
🕐 Mon **W** habutosf.com · $$
A great Japanese restaurant – the sashimi melts in the mouth.

4. Good Luck Dim Sum
D3 🏠 736 Clement St **W** good-luck-dim-sum.res-menu.com · $
This tiny place has a wide selection of inexpensive dim sum. The chive-and-shrimp dumplings are especially good. Perfect for take out.

5. Chapeau!
C3 🏠 126 Clement St at 2nd Ave
🕐 L **W** chapeausf.com · $$
A memorably quaint French bistro. The sommelier can direct you to fine wines that pair well with the classic fare, which includes filet mignon.

6. Outerlands
A3 🏠 4001 Judah St
W outerlandssf.com · $
Grab a table outside, or enjoy the rustic interior, here. Feast on the creative, organic-based menus, offering fresh seafood, veggie soups and sandwiches, along with salads. They serve great cocktails, too. Come early for the popular weekend brunch.

PRICE CATEGORIES
For a three-course meal for one with half a bottle of wine (or equivalent meal), taxes, and extra charges.

$ under $50 $$ $50–$100
$$$ over $100

7. Pizzetta 211
C3 🏠 211 23rd Ave
W pizzetta211.com · $
Thin and crisp pizza topped with organic ingredients from fragrant aioli to homemade sausage.

8. Café Bunn Mi
D3 🏠 417 Clement St **W** cafe-bunn-mi.restaurants-world.com · $
Vietnamese sandwiches at their best, and for a bargain, too.

9. Java Beach Café
A5 🏠 1396 La Playa St
W javabeachcafe.com · $
This cozy café serves sandwiches, soups, and pastries in a nautical-themed interior.

10. Burma Superstar
D3 🏠 309 Clement St
W burmasuperstar.com · $
This Burmese restaurant features an extensive menu of flavorsome noodles, curries, and salads.

Delicious brunch dishes at Outerlands

HONNEUR ET PATRIE

Clockwise from above
**Rodin's *The Thinker*
at the Legion of
Honor museum;
Old Master gallery
in the museum;
The Bath by Jean-
Léon Gérôme**

THE BAY AREA

In local parlance, the Bay Area includes the city, the East Bay, Marin County, the Peninsula, and the South Bay. Although Santa Clara, San Jose, Santa Cruz, and Capitola do not touch the waters of the Bay, they embody the same open-minded ethos that defines it. This is largely due to Northern California's well-known liberal population and diverse community. In towns such as Berkeley, the emphasis is on progressive thinking and student life, while smaller enclaves such as Bolinas live life in harmony with the breathtaking nature all around them. Once a focus for Spanish missions and Gold Rush prospectors, the area is best known now for its relaxed lifestyle, liberal politics, and high-tech industry.

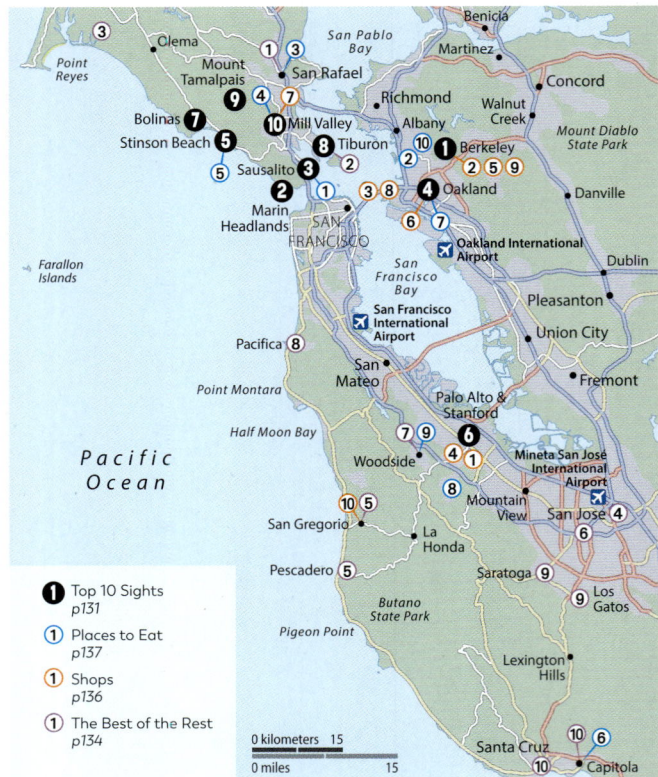

Top 10 Sights
p131

Places to Eat
p137

Shops
p136

The Best of the Rest
p134

For places to stay in this area, see p151

**Attractive Bayside hamlet
of Sausalito**

1 Berkeley

Known as "Berzerkeley," for the student dissent of the 1960s, today the tree-shaded UC Berkeley campus is still the center of TV-worthy protests. As one of the world's greatest universities, "Cal's" faculty features many Nobel laureates. This diversity-proud East Bay city is full of gourmet cafés and a variety of restaurants. Fourth street is sprinkled with shops, while the parks, as well as the biking and hiking trails, appeal to those wishing to escape the bustle of city life.

2 Marin Headlands

To visit these raw, wild hills with astonishingly beautiful views is to enter another world; yet it's only half an hour's drive from the city, via the Golden Gate Bridge. The scale of the rolling terrain is immense, and the precipitous drops into the ocean are dramatic. This is an unspoiled area of wildlife (Point Reyes to the north is home to tule elk herds), wind-swept ridges, sheltered valleys, and deserted beaches (*p66*).

3 Sausalito

A former fishing community and now an upscale commuter area and tourist haven, this small town offers spectacular views of San Francisco from its Bridgeway Avenue promenade. Historically, it has been an artists' town, home to an eccentric mix of residents.

Bungalows cling to the hillsides and boats fill the picturesque marinas, many of which are houseboats that locals live in year-round. There are excellent restaurants, places to stay, and some unique shopping possibilities, too.

4 Oakland

Oakland is a multicultural haven for artists and musicians. The city's attractions include the huge Lake Merritt, which offers a range of recreational possibilities, the Oakland Museum of California (*p56*), the Oakland Zoo, two glorious Art Deco-era theaters (Paramount and Fox), the Jack London Square waterfront complex of restaurants and stores, the USS *Potomac* (FDR's Floating White House), and a ferry landing. In the hills, you will find a beautiful Mormon Temple, with dazzling Bay views, the Redwood Regional Park, and the Chabot Space and Science Center.

**Lovely interior of the
Fox Theater, Oakland**

GREAT BAY AREA UNIVERSITIES

Palo Alto's Stanford University is the Bay Area's most famous private institution of higher learning, inaugurated in 1891. However, in terms of intellectual clout, the University of California at Berkeley, the oldest campus in the California system, stands shoulder to shoulder, considering the number of Nobel laureates on the faculty and its international importance.

5 Stinson Beach
Hwy 1

Since the early 20th century, this has been a popular vacation spot and remains the preferred swimming beach for the whole area. The soft sand and spectacular sunsets set off the quaint village, with its good restaurants and interesting stores. You can reach it via the coast route, but the drive up Highway 1 gives the most dramatic arrival, with inspiring views as you exit the forest onto the headlands.

6 Palo Alto and Stanford
Hwys 101 & 82

An erstwhile sleepy university town, Palo Alto has experienced a boom as the focal point of Silicon Valley and driving force of the "New Economy." The town has been left with a considerably dressed-up appearance, as well as many fancy restaurants, hotels, and stores. It's also home to the prestigious Stanford University *(p90)*, with its beautiful, well-tended campus.

7 Bolinas
Hwy 1

Bolinas is a hippie village that time forgot. Its citizens regularly take down road signs showing the way to downtown, to keep visitors away. Potters and other craftspeople sell their wares in the funky gallery, organic produce and vegetarianism are the rule, and 1960s idealism still predominates.

8 Tiburon
Hwy 131

Marin County's less hectic alternative to Sausalito – here, 100-year-old houseboats ("arks") have been pulled ashore and refurbished, forming "Ark Row." It houses stores, restaurants, and cafés that enhance the charm of this waterfront village. There are also opportunities to see wildlife in the parks along the shore, facing Angel Island and the city.

Exploring the campus at Stanford University

Hiking trail in Muir Woods, Mount Tamalpais

9 Mount Tamalpais
⌂ Hwy 1

From the summit of 2,570-ft (785-m) "Mount Tam," sacred to the Indigenous people who once lived here, practically the entire Bay Area can be seen. The area is a State Park, with more than 200 miles (320 km) of trails through redwood groves.

10 Mill Valley
⌂ Off Hwy 101

Home to a well-known film festival, this is the quintessential Marin County town; wealthy, relaxed, beautiful, and with a well-educated populace. The old part of town is flanked by redwoods, lined with old buildings housing restaurants and unusual stores, and the whole area centers around an eternally pleasant public square.

A MORNING WALK AROUND BERKELEY

Begin at UC Berkeley's **Koret Visitor Center** on Piedmont Avenue at Bancroft Way, where you can pick up information and maps. Continue on Piedmont Ave to the **Hearst Greek Theatre**, an excellent concert venue. Then go left on University Drive; on your left, you'll shortly come across the Campanile Esplanade, which leads to the main campus landmark, the 307-ft (94-m) **Sather Tower**, also known as the Campanile, based on the famous bell tower in Venice's Piazza San Marco.

From the tower, Campanile Way leads to Harmon Way, bringing you to the Neo-Romanesque **Wellman Hall**. From here, University Drive and then Crescent Lawn follow along the Eucalyptus Grove or Grinnel Natural area. Cross Oxford to find the **Berkeley Art Museum and Pacific Film Archive**. Head back through the Eucalyptus Grove to Fran Schelssinger Way. A roundabout will take you to Grade Street and then Sather's Cross Path, leading to Sather Gate and then into **Sproul Plaza,** epicenter of the student Free Speech Movement of the 1960s. Exit the campus onto Telegraph Avenue. One block over is **People's Park.**

After your walk, head over to **The Cheese Board Collective** (*cheese boardcollective.coop*). The restaurant serves one type of vegetarian pizza a day, and is known for its wide selection of rare cheeses.

Winchester Mystery House surrounded by its lush gardens

The Best of the Rest

1. San Rafael
⌂ Hwy 101

This town has a charming historic center with good restaurants and shops. A farmers' market transforms the main drag into a bustling hub every Thursday evening.

2. Belvedere Island

This garden island, attached by a causeway to Tiburon, is one of the Bay's most exclusive residential areas. It's worth a visit to see the palatial homes and their sumptuous setting.

3. Point Reyes
⌂ Hwy 1 to Olema, then signposted to Point Reyes

This windswept peninsula is a haven for wildlife, including a herd of tule elk; it is also home to cattle ranches. You can watch migrating whales offshore from December to March.

4. San Jose
⌂ Hwy 101

This sprawling town is an integral part of Silicon Valley enterprises and has popular attractions.

5. San Gregorio and Pescadero
⌂ Hwy 1

San Gregorio Private Beach is the Bay Area's oldest nude beach. It is adjacent to the Pescadero State Beach, which has lots of tide pools. The fishing village evokes the Old West, complete with a whitewashed wooden church. Duarte's Tavern has been serving artichoke soup and olallieberry pie since 1894.

6. Winchester Mystery House
⌂ 525 S Winchester Blvd, San Jose ⓦ winchestermystery house.com ⚡

The eccentric 19th-century home of the rifle heiress, Sarah Winchester, took 38 years to build and includes stairways leading to nowhere and windows set into floors.

7. Woodside
⌂ Hwy 280

This bucolic residential area is where many of the first families to have lived in the Bay Area built fabulous mansions in the late 19th century.

8. Pacifica
⌂ Hwy 1 off Hwy 280

A popular weekend destination, this oceanfront city is great for surfing, fishing, cycling, golf, and hiking. Lodgings and seafood restaurants face the ocean, and the quaint little downtown is lined with stores.

9. Los Gatos and Saratoga
⌂ Hwy 85

These tree-lined small towns, full of restaurants and stores, have become upscale communities for the movers and shakers of Silicon Valley.

10. Santa Cruz and Capitola
⌂ Hwy 1

Enjoy some of the Central Coast's best swimming, plus the Boardwalk, a famous vintage amusement park.

Oakland Museum of California

1. Earthquake Artifacts
A collection of objects that pertain to the terrible earthquake of 1906 is on display here, including porcelain cups and saucers fused together by the heat of the fire that destroyed so much of the city.

2. Natural Sciences
In the brilliant Gallery of California Natural Sciences, the state is presented as one of the world's top 10 biological "hot spots." There are thousands of artifacts on display, including bird and mammal study skins and mounts, as well as an enormous collection of reptiles, amphibians, and fungi.

3. Mission-Era Artifacts
A 19th-century icon of St. Peter is just one remnant of the Spanish Mission years you'll find here, where there are also colonial tools and part of a Spanish ship.

4. The Earliest Californians
Fascinating galleries explore early human history in the state of California, documented by materials such as basketry, stone tools, clothing, and objects used in rituals.

5. Gold Rush Artifacts
The lives of those who came to California from all over the world in the 19th century, hoping to strike it rich, are chronicled here. You'll see gold nuggets, prospecting tools, and rare mining equipment.

6. Californian History
This section of the museum has exhibits associated with technology, agriculture, business, and domestic life from the early Indigenous people up to the 21st century. Subjects such as World War II, baby boomers, Hollywood, and Silicon Valley are also covered.

7. The Building
The museum building is an outstanding example of modern design. Opened in 1969, it is composed of reinforced concrete and consists of three levels of tiered terraces. To soften its angularity, roof gardens have been planted, accented with sculpture.

8. Art Gallery
The third level of the museum is devoted to the Gallery of California Art, featuring works by artists who have studied, lived, and worked here. Included are works by California Impressionists and members of the Bay Area Figurative Movement. Check the website *(museumca.org)* for the opening times of the California Art and History galleries.

9. Photography
The Gallery of California Art also has an impressive collection of the work of California photographers, including Ansel Adams, Edward Weston, and Dorothea Lange.

10. Californian Crafts
This is the largest collection in the world of work by California Arts and Crafts practitioners Arthur and Lucia Kleinhans Mathews, including paintings, drawings, furniture, and other decorative art.

Objects brought by the Spaniards to California on display

Shops

1. Stanford Shopping Center
📍 660 Stanford Shopping Center, Palo Alto Ⓦ simon.com/mall/stanford-shopping-center

One of the first shopping centers in the Bay Area, this outdoor mall is dog-friendly and features stores that you don't tend to find everywhere, such as Hermès Paris, Free People, and Bloomingdale's.

2. Favor
📍 1649 San Pablo Ave, Berkeley Ⓦ shopatfavor.com

Beautifully carved resin jewelry and exclusive Hotcakes Design by designer Caramia are stocked at Favor along with works from designers across the globe.

3. Gene Hiller
📍 729 Bridgeway Ave, Sausalito Ⓦ genehiller.com

Since 1953, this menswear store has been offering the finest imported designer clothing – from classic formal to casual – including Ermenegildo Zegna and Canali.

4. Shady Lane
📍 325 Sharon Park Dr, Menlo Park Ⓦ shadylanegallery.com

This boutique was founded by a collective of artists who wanted to create a showcase for their designs in areas like jewelry and ceramics. It's full of unique pieces and nice gifts.

5. Moe's Books
📍 2476 Telegraph Ave, Berkeley Ⓦ moesbooks.com

Opened by Moe Moskowitz in 1959, Moe's Books offers an excellent selection of new, used, and rare books.

6. Oaklandish
📍 1444 Broadway, Oakland Ⓦ oaklandish.com

Established as a public art project in 2000, Oaklandish creates unique clothing while supporting the local community.

7. Margaret O'Leary
📍 14 Miller Ave, Mill Valley Ⓦ margaretoleary.com

Mill Valley is home to the flagship store of this women's knitwear label, known for its classic, upscale takes on California comfort.

8. Heath Ceramics
📍 500 Gate 5 Rd, Sausalito Ⓦ heathceramics.com

An iconic Bay Area ceramics studio and store, Heath Ceramics features mid-century modern dinnerware, home accents, and imperfect factory pieces sold at reduced rates.

9. Fourth Street
📍 Berkeley 📞 (510) 644-3002

A tree-shaded warren of boutiques and galleries, this popular street is lined by the likes of The Gardener, Sur La Table, Stained Glass Garden, Builders Booksource, and Five Little Monkeys.

10. San Gregorio Store
📍 7615 Stage Rd Ⓦ sangregoriostore.com

Near San Gregorio State Beach, this store has a Wild West vibe, featuring a collection of curiosities and unique gifts. It has live music on weekends.

Browsing homeware items at Heath Ceramics

Places to Eat

**Wide range of cakes at
Gayle's Bakery and Rosticceria**

1. Poggio Trattoria
🏠 777 Bridgeway, Sausalito
Ⓦ poggiotrattoria.com · $$
Overlooking the waterfront, this trattoria serves award-winning Northern Italian food. There is also a list of fabulous cocktails on offer. Grab a booth or a sidewalk table.

2. Viks Chaat
🏠 2390 Fourth Street, Berkeley
Ⓦ vikschaat.com · $
This big, lively restaurant attached to a South Asian grocery store serves excellent Indian street food.

3. Sol Food
🏠 901 Lincoln Ave, San Rafael
Ⓦ solfoodrestaurant.com · $
Line up for a taste of the flavorful, festive Puerto Rican food at this restaurant. There is a special dish on the menu, which changes every day.

4. The Depot Café and Bookstore
🏠 87 Throckmorton Ave, Mill Valley
Ⓦ depotcafeandbookstore.com · $
This bookstore, with its renowned café, offers regular author events as well as phenomenal paninis.

5. Parkside Snack Bar
🏠 43 Arenal Ave, Stinson Beach
Ⓦ parksidecafe.com · $
Creative brunch at picnic tables on the patio, or in the dining room.

6. Gayle's Bakery and Rosticceria
🏠 504 Bay Ave, Capitola
Ⓦ gaylesbakery.com · $
This bakery and *rosticceria* (or deli) features an extraordinary selection of gourmet treats, both sweet and savory. Try the Princess Cake and the to-die-for cupcakes.

7. Cafe Eritrea D'Afrique
🏠 4069 Telegraph Ave, Oahland
Ⓦ cafeeritreadafrique.com · $
An acclaimed restaurant serving Eritrean and Ethiopian cuisine in a relaxing and friendly atmosphere.

8. Alpine Inn
🏠 3915 Alpine Rd, Portola Valley
Ⓦ alpineinnpv.com · $
In a building that dates back to 1850, this greasy beer bar with a garden is popular with locals and Silicon Valley workers alike for its substantial burgers and fries.

9. Buck's
🏠 3062 Woodside Drive, Woodside
Ⓦ buckswoodside.com · $
After a long hike on one of the many trails in Woodside, enjoy a hearty short rib hash and coffee at this restaurant.

10. Chez Panisse
🏠 1517 Shattuck Ave, Berkeley
🕐 Sun Ⓦ chezpanisse.com · $$$
A popular Berkeley spot, Chez Panisse has been serving up excellent California cuisine, using organic seasonal ingredients, since 1971. The upstairs café offers a cheaper alternative.

STREETSMART

Sightseeing aboard a cable car

GETTING AROUND

Whether you are exploring San Francisco on foot or using public transportation, here is everything you need to know to navigate the city and the areas beyond the center like a pro.

AT A GLANCE

PUBLIC TRANSPORTATION COSTS
Tickets are valid on all Muni-operated public transportation options.

SINGLE TICKET

$2.75

120 minutes of travel on Muni

1-DAY PASSPORT

$14.00

Unlimited travel for one day

7-DAY PASSPORT

$44.00

Unlimited travel for seven days

SPEED LIMIT

RURAL FREEWAYS

65 mph
(105 km/h)

URBAN FREEWAYS

65 mph
(105 km/h)

NEIGHBORHOOD SLOW ZONES

20 mph
(30 km/h)

URBAN AREAS

35 mph
(55 km/h)

Arriving by Air

San Francisco International Airport (SFO) is 14 miles (23 km) south of the city. It is one of the world's busiest airports, with connections to and from the Pacific Rim, Latin America and Europe. Visitors will arrive at SFO on the lower level. The top level provides services for onward travel to the city center. For a list of transportation options, see the table opposite. The Bay Area Rapid Transit (BART) station is connected to the terminals by a light-rail shuttle.

Other nearby airports include **San José Mineta International Airport** (SJC), which is about an hour away from San Francisco, and **Oakland International Airport** (OAK), which is 30 minutes away. Both airports are connected to San Francisco by buses and BART.

San Jose Mineta International Airport
W flysanjose.com
Oakland International Airport
W oaklandairport.com
San Francisco International Airport
W flysfo.com

Train Travel

Amtrak trains link most major US cities. Advance booking is recommended. Those visiting San Francisco by train will arrive at the station in Emeryville. From here, a shuttle takes you to downtown San Francisco.

Alternatively, you can travel by Amtrak to San Jose, then transfer via the **CalTrain** commuter rail system to San Francisco. A separate ticket is required for this journey.

Amtrak
W amtrak.com
CalTrain
W caltrain.org

Long-Distance Bus Travel

For travelers on a budget and with more time, buses are a great option. **Greyhound** buses take passengers from Los Angeles to San Francisco in around nine hours from $38. The **Green Tortoise** bus company offers a unique way to see California, stopping at sights.

Green Tortoise
W greentortoise.com

Greyhound
W greyhound.com

Public Transportation

San Francisco has a transportation system run by the San Francisco Municipal Transportation Agency (**SFMTA**). The city's bus and Metro network is known as the Muni and covers buses, light-rail Metro trains, streetcars (electric trams), and cable cars. The San Francisco Peninsula and the East Bay are linked by **BART** trains. This is an efficient way to get to both SFO and OAK. Timetables, ticket information, transportation maps, and more can be obtained from the SFMTA website.

BART
W bart.gov

SFMTA
W sfmta.com

Planning Your Journey

Public transportation is busiest at 7am–9am and 4pm–7pm from Monday through Friday. The cable cars are a popular tourist activity, so are busy during the summer months. The Muni Metro runs from around 5am to 1am on weekdays, from 7am on Saturdays and 8am on Sundays. There are 10 Muni Owl services that run 24 hours a day, seven days a week. Schedules are modified for public holidays.

Tickets

The **Clipper card** app, which can be downloaded and used on a smart phone, is the most convenient way to plan your journey and to purchase digital tickets. Or, you can purchase a reusable Clipper card from Muni Metro stations or from Walgreens stores for just $3. You can top the card up with money and use it to travel on the Muni, BART, and cable cars.

Muni passports are available for 1, 3, or 7 days, allowing unlimited travel. These can be purchased from the Visitor Information Center (*p84*), the kiosk at San Francisco Airport, and at other stores throughout the city.

Clipper Card
W clippercard.com

Buses

There are bus stops every two or three blocks. Bus shelters list the route number of the buses that stop there. Most have digital signs showing when the next bus will arrive. Route numbers followed by a letter are either express services or make limited stops. You can pay with exact change, or show your Muni Passport or Clipper card.

Metro

The Metro light-rail system operates both above and below ground. Lines J (Church), K (Ingleside), L (Taraval), M (Ocean View), N (Judah), and T (Third) share the same tracks, so check the letter and name of the vehicle when boarding from Market Street. To go west, follow signs indicating "Outbound"; to go east, choose "Downtown."

Streetcars

The F-Line streetcar runs along Market Street only, and has vintage streetcars from all over the world. While these streetcars are scenic, they're not the best option if you're in a rush.

GETTING TO AND FROM THE AIRPORT

Transport	Journey Time	Price
Taxi	25-45 minutes	$45
SuperShuttle shared ride	40-60 minutes	$19-$50
American Airporter Shuttle	60-75 minutes	$17
Bay Area Rapid Transit (BART)	30 minutes	$9.65

Cable Cars

San Francisco's cable cars are world-famous, and even classed as a "moving national monument." Service runs every 10 minutes from 6am to midnight daily; the fare is $8 per journey, with a discount for seniors and those with disabilities after 9pm and before 7am. There are three routes: the Powell-Hyde line, which passes Union Square and climbs Nob Hill, providing good views of Chinatown; the Powell-Mason line begins in the same place and branches off to pass North Beach, ending at Bay Street (sit facing east for the best views); and the California line runs from the base of Market Street at the Embarcadero, through the Financial District and Chinatown, over Nob Hill, ending at Van Ness Avenue.

BART

BART trains run from 5am on weekdays, from 6am on Saturdays, and from 8am on Sundays, until around midnight. Tickets are issued by machines in BART stations. You must present your ticket at the turnstile both when you board and leave the train. You can also use a Clipper card. The final destination of the train will be displayed on the front of the train itself, and the direction of travel will be marked on the platform.

Taxis

Taxis in San Francisco operate 24 hours a day. They are licensed and regulated, so expect efficient service, expert local knowledge, and a set price. A taxi will have its rooftop sign illuminated when vacant. It will also display the company name and phone number, plus the cab number. Make a note of these, and if you leave anything in the cab, call the company and quote the cab number.

To catch a cab, wait at a taxi stand, call and request a pick-up, or hail a vacant cab. Tell your driver your exact destination. The meter will be on the dashboard; expect to add a 15 to 20 percent tip to the final amount. Fares are often posted inside the cab. There

is usually a flat fee of around $4.15 for the first mile (1.6 km). This increases by about $3.25 for each additional mile, or 65 cents per minute while waiting. The driver will write a receipt on request. If you travel 15 miles (24 km) or more beyond the city limits, the fare will be 150 percent of the metered rate.

The ride share companies Uber and Lyft are very cost-effective and reliable in San Francisco; download the apps onto your smartphone. It is advisable not to take a limousine from the street. Legally, limousines are only available for prearranged trips.

Driving

Congestion, a shortage of parking spaces, and strictly enforced laws discourage many visitors from driving in San Francisco, but possibly the best way to experience the twists and turns of Lombard Street is on four wheels.

Car Rental

To rent a car you must be at least 25 years old with a valid driving license. Most agencies require a large deposit. It is slightly cheaper to rent a car from the airport. It is also more cost effective to do a round trip, to avoid large drop-off costs. Check your existing insurance policy before signing up to car insurance, as you may already be covered.

Rules of the Road

Many streets are one-way, with traffic lights at most corners. In California, if there is no oncoming traffic, drivers may turn right at a red light, always giving pedestrians the right of way. Otherwise, a red light means stop, and an amber means proceed with caution.

Parking

Parking meters operate 9am to 6pm Monday through Saturday, except on national holidays, when parking is free. Meters in some tourist areas operate on Sundays, including at Fisherman's Wharf and the Embarcadero. Meter time limits vary and costs range from $2 to $6 per hour. You can prepay from 4:30am online with the **PaybyPhone** website. City-center parking garages are also available from $16 per day.

Curbs here are color-coded. A red curb means no stopping; yellow means a commercial loading zone; green allows 10 to 30 minutes of parking; and white allows you to park for five minutes during business hours, with the driver remaining in the vehicle. Blue-curb areas are reserved for those with disabilities. By law, you must curb your wheels when parking on steep hills. Turn your wheels into the road when your car is parked facing uphill, and toward the curb when facing downhill. Check signs for tow warnings and follow all instructions.

PaybyPhone
W m2.paybyphone.com/parking

Penalties

If you park your car at an out-of-order meter, expect to get a parking ticket. Blocking bus stops, fire hydrants, driveways, garages, and wheelchair ramps will also incur a fine, as will running a red light or a stop sign, or texting while driving.

Driving Outside the City

No toll payment is required to leave the city, but you will need to pay between $7 and $9.40 to reenter. During rush hour, cars with multiple occupants can use the carpool lane, avoiding both traffic and tolls. It is legal to drive in the carpool lane when it's not rush hour, but not to avoid the bridge tolls. Those caught using the carpool lane illegally face steep fines.

Cycling

Cycling is popular in San Francisco. There are many bicycle lanes and all Muni buses are equipped to carry bikes on the outside. Bikes can also be taken on the Muni light-rail cars and on BART, although not at rush hour. There are two marked scenic bicycle routes.

One goes from Golden Gate park south to Lake Merced; the other starts at the southern end of the Golden Gate Bridge and crosses to Marin County.

Bicycles, equipment, and tours are available to book from **Bay City Bike** and **Blazing Saddles**. They rent out bikes from $8 per hour, $36 ($25 for children) per day, or $105 for seven days.

Bay City Bike
W baycitybike.com
Blazing Saddles
W blazingsaddles.com

Walking

Compact and gridded, San Francisco is entirely walkable. Downtown and the Mission, in particular, are forgivingly flat, while Nob Hill and Russian Hill reward steep climbs with spectacular views. It's a little more arduous out on the avenues of Richmond and Sunset, but walking is a good way to get a feel for each neighborhood.

Boats and Ferries

Ferries are one of the best ways to appreciate the beauty of the Bay Area. They shuttle to and from the cities of San Francisco, Oakland, and Larkspur, as well as the smaller towns of Tiburon and Sausalito, and nearby Angel Island. Viewing the coastline from the ferry is less expensive than a sightseeing cruise. The trip from San Francisco to Sausalito is $14.25 (children and seniors $8.50) each way. These ferries only carry foot passengers and bicycles. **Golden Gate Ferry** and **San Francisco Bay Ferry** services depart from the Ferry Building, and the **Blue and Gold Fleet** and **Red and White Fleet** dock at Fisherman's Wharf.

Blue and Gold Fleet
W blueandgoldfleet.com
Golden Gate Ferry
W goldengate.org
Red and White Fleet
W redandwhite.com
San Francisco Bay Ferry
W sanfranciscobayferry.com

PRACTICAL INFORMATION

A little local know-how goes a long way in San Francisco. On these pages you can find all the essential advice and information you will need to make the most of your trip to this city.

AT A GLANCE

CURRENCY
US dollar (USD)

AVERAGE DAILY SPEND

SAVE	SPEND	SPLURGE
$150	$250	$350+

BOTTLED WATER	COFFEE	BEER	DINNER FOR TWO
$2.50	$3.50	$7.00	$90

CLIMATE

Apr to Aug average 14 hours of sunlight, dropping to under 10 from Nov to Feb.

Temperatures average less than 65°F/18°C in summer and 50°F/10°C in winter.

It rarely rains from Feb to Nov, while fog can roll in any day.

ELECTRICITY SUPPLY

Plug sockets are type A and B, fitting two- and three-pronged plugs. Standard voltage is 100–120 volts AC.

Passports and Visas

For entry requirements, including visas, consult your nearest US embassy or check the **US Department of State** website. Canadians typically do not require a visa to enter the US, although there are some exceptions. Citizens of Australia, New Zealand, the UK, or the EU do not need a visa, but must apply in advance for the Electronic System for Travel Authorization (**ESTA**). There is a small charge for this service. All other visitors need to obtain a visa in advance of traveling. A return airline ticket is required to enter the country.

ESTA
W esta.cbp.dhs.gov
US Department of State
W travel.state.gov

Government Advice

Now more than ever, it is important to consult both your and the US governments' advice before traveling. The US Department of State, the UK Foreign, Commonwealth and Development Office (**FCDO**), and the **Australian Department of Foreign Affairs and Trade** offer the latest information on security, health, and local regulations.

Australian Department of Foreign Affairs and Trade
W smartraveller.gov.au
FCDO
W gov.uk/foreign-travel-advice

Customs Information

You can find information on the laws relating to goods and currency taken in or out of the United States on the **US Customs and Border Protection** website. You are allowed to bring in 1.75 pints (1 liter) of wine or liquor, 200 cigarettes, 100 cigars, and $100 worth of gifts. Certain fruits and vegetables, animals, and animal products are not allowed. You may carry up to $10,000 in US or foreign currency out of or into the country; larger sums must

be declared, which entails filing a FinCEN Form 105.
US Customs and Border Protection
W cbp.gov

Insurance
We recommend taking out a comprehensive insurance policy covering theft, loss of belongings, medical care, cancellations and delays, and read the fine print carefully. The US healthcare system is predominantly private – and expensive– so it is essential to ensure medical cover.

Vaccinations
No inoculations are required when visiting the US.

Money
Most establishments accept major credit, debit, and prepaid currency cards. Contactless payments are widespread. You are never far from an ATM in the city, though you may be charged $2.50 to $3.50 per transaction in addition to any ATM withdrawal fees. To avoid these fees, make a purchase in a store using a debit card and ask for cash.

Cash is still used by some smaller businesses and street vendors, and most retailers will accept cash payments. Currency can be exchanged at any of the three international airports, at Downtown banks and hotels, as well as at bureaux de change.

Tax (around 10 percent), service charge (around 20 percent), and an SF mandate charge are often added to a restaurant bill. A useful way to figure out an appropriate restaurant tip is to double the tax. In hotels, it is a general custom to tip porters $1.50 per bag and housekeeping $2 per night.

Travelers with Specific Requirements
Disabled access is extensive throughout San Francisco, from ramped curbs for wheelchairs to telecommunication devices for hearing-impaired travelers. However, the city is famous for its steep hills, particularly around Russian Hill and Nob Hill, which may prove challenging for those who have mobility issues.

Public transportation is largely accessible for those with specific requirements, and prices are usually discounted. The free Muni Access Guide to public transportation is available on the SFMTA website *(p141)* and **Access Northern California** provides information on accessible travel and recreation in San Francisco, the Bay Area, and beyond. Information about the accessibility of parks, trails, and places of interest along California's coast, including the areas around San Francisco, can be found on **Wheeling Cal's Coast**.
Access Northern California
W accessnca.org
Wheeling Cal's Coast
W wheelingcalscoast.org

Language
The official language of San Francisco is English, but more than a hundred languages are spoken in the city. Spanish and Chinese are well established as second and third languages.

Opening Hours
Museums and attractions are generally open daily, but always check individual websites before visiting.

Shops are generally open daily from 10am to 5pm and often later. Some groceries, drugstores, and supermarkets are open daily from 7am to 11pm. Chain stores and malls often open on holidays.

Banks are open from 9am to 5pm Monday to Friday, and some are open on weekends.

Situations can change quickly and unexpectedly. Always check before visiting attractions and hospitality venues for up-to-date opening hours and booking requirements.

Personal Security

San Francisco is one of the safest large cities in the US. Police patrol tourist areas frequently, and few visitors become victims of street crime. That said, it is always advisable to take the usual precautions against petty crime and be alert to your surroundings. The city is experiencing a housing crisis and thousands of people are living in encampments, which has unfortunately led to a rise in petty crime. Tackling this issue is a priority for the local government, but it may take some years before things visibly improve.

San Francisco is at risk of earthquakes and wildfires. Should you experience a quake, there are simple safety rules to follow. If indoors, crouch under a table or doorway, away from windows and wall hangings, and hold on until the shaking stops. If outdoors, stay away from power cables and trees. If driving, pull over, away from power lines and bridges, and remain in the car. If you're on the beach, move to higher ground. The Federal Emergency Management Agency (**FEMA**) has a website with useful information about safety measures, and you can also access a California-wide early warning system through the free **MyShake** app. The **Department of Forestry and Fire Protection** website has maps showing the locations of any wildfires. The peak wildfire season is from July to October when hot, dry winds are most frequent.

As a general rule, San Franciscans are very accepting of all people, regardless of their race, gender, or sexuality. California recognized the rights of those wanting to legally change their gender in the mid-1980s and same-sex marriage was legalized in 2008. San Francisco has an incredibly diverse LGBTQ+ community, with a history stretching back to the Gold Rush. If you do feel unsafe, the **Safe Space Alliance** pinpoints your nearest place of refuge.

Department of Forestry and Fire Protection
W fire.ca.gov

FEMA
W fema.gov

MyShake
W myshake.berkeley.edu

Safe Space Alliance
W safespacealliance.com

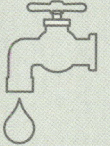

Health

Healthcare in the US is high quality but costly. Ensure you have full medical cover prior to your visit, and keep receipts to claim on your insurance.

Walgreens pharmacies are all over the city, and branches at 498 Castro Street, 135 Powell Street, Divisadero Street, and Westborough Square are open 24 hours. Certain medications available over the counter elsewhere require a prescription in the US.

Smoking, Alcohol, and Drugs

You must be at least 21 to buy and drink alcohol, and to buy tobacco products. It is legal for those 21 and over to smoke marijuana in the home or in a building licensed for its consumption. Drinking alcohol is not allowed in most public areas, especially from open containers. Driving while under the influence of alcohol or any drug is prohibited. It is illegal to smoke in public buildings, workplaces, restaurants, and bars. It is also illegal to smoke anywhere that exposes others to secondhand smoke, including parks, beaches, and bus stops. These laws extend to e-cigarettes.

ID

Take a form of photo identification when buying alcohol, tobacco, or marijuana, as bars, clubs, restaurants, and shops are required by law to check it.

Cell Phones and Wi-Fi

Cell phone service in San Francisco is excellent. The main US network providers are AT&T, Sprint, T-Mobile US, and Verizon. Most of these offer prepaid, pay-as-you-go phones and US SIM cards, starting at around $30 (plus tax). Calls within the US are cheap, but making international calls may be pricey. Any triband or multiband cell phone should work in the US.

Wi-Fi is free at the airports and at cafés and lodgings, as well as on some public transportation, including trains. You can also access free Wi-Fi in public spaces by connecting to #SFWiFi.

Post

Stamps can be bought from post offices, drugstores, and newsstands. On-street mailboxes are usually blue.

Taxes

Sales tax in San Francisco is 8.5 percent. Tax is charged on everything except groceries, plants used for food, and prescription drugs, with a few other exemptions.

Discount Cards

Several websites, including **Sightseeing Pass** and **CityPASS**, offer discounts and passes, often grouping together attractions and public transportation. Visitors with proof of student status receive discounts at many museums and theaters.

CityPASS
W citypass.com
Sightseeing Pass
W sightseeingpass.com

Trips and Tours

Taking an organized trip or tour is a popular way to get around and see the city. The choice of such tours is plentiful. **Big Bus San Francisco** offers multi-lingual, hop-on-hop-off, open-top bus tours of the main sights of the city. **San Francisco Whale Tours** sail under the Golden Gate Bridge to a vast marine sanctuary to see whales and sea turtles. **Alcatraz Cruises** offer narrated ferry rides and a multilingual audio walking tour of the island. For free walking tours of the city led by locals and historians, try **San Francisco City Guides**. **Edible Excursions** offer culinary strolls through different areas.

Alcatraz Cruises
W alcatrazcruises.com
Big Bus San Francisco
W eng.bigbustours.com
Edible Excursions
W edibleexcursions.net
San Francisco City Guides
W sfcityguides.org
San Francisco Whale Tours
W sanfranciscowhaletours.com

PLACES TO STAY

San Francisco's accommodations range from cozy and affordable hostels to grand Victorian B&Bs. The best area to stay depends on the experience you want: Fisherman's Wharf is great for first-timers looking for easy access to the top sights while the Mission District is full of buzzy bars and restaurants.

The city has mild weather year-round, but August to October offers the sunniest days; November to March, meanwhile, is the rainiest season. Hotels charge a 14 percent tax for temporary stays.

PRICE CATEGORIES

For a standard double room per night (with breakfast if included) including taxes and extra charges

$ under $200
$$ $200–$300
$$$ over $300

Downtown

Beacon Grand
G2 **450 Powell St**
W beacongrand.com · **$$**

This historic hotel was first opened in 1928 as The Sir Francis Drake, but after a careful restoration, it is now enjoying a new life as the Beacon Grand. The hotel is designed to celebrate San Francisco's heritage and has nods to its Roaring Twenties past like the Prohibition-themed Hidden Library bar and glitzy gold accents in the rooms. A stay here is a stylish treat.

Green Tortoise Hostel
H1 **494 Broadway**
W greentortoisesf.com · **$**

A short walking distance from Chinatown, Union Square, and Fisherman's Wharf, this friendly hostel is a great budget option in the heart of the city. With added perks like a grand ballroom common space with pool tables and foosball, live music and an on-site sauna, the Green Tortoise is a great option for social travelers.

The Clancy
H3 **299 2nd St**
W marriott.com/en-us/hotels/sfoaw-the-clancy-autograph-collection · **$$$**

The Clancy is nestled in the SoMA neighborhood and is just as bright and vibrant as its environs. The common spaces are decorated with artworks by local artists and the rooms are as colorful as they are comfortable. With its location right by the SFMOMA and Chase Center, it's a great place to retreat to after exploring in the city.

Hotel Nikko
G3 **222 Mason St**
W hotelnikhosf.com · **$$**

This Union Square-based, Japan-inspired hotel is a luxurious city-center stay. With decor reminiscent of cherry blossoms and a cool blue color scheme, Hotel Nikko transports guests to a peaceful oasis. Not to mention it is one of the few places in the city to serve authentic Japanese breakfasts, complete with broiled fish, miso soup, and sliced pickles at the hotel's fabulous Restaurant Anzu.

Hotel Zelos
G3 **12 4th St**
W hotelssf.com/zelos · **$$**

This sleek Downtown hotel embraces a fashion-forward aesthetic. But don't let the sharp angles and steely gray walls fool you – comfort is top of mind here, and the rooms deliver it in spades. As an added plus, the hotel's Dirty Habit bar, a long-time favorite with locals, has a cool, grungy vibe and a unique cocktail list.

Hostelling International
G3 **312 Mason St**
W hiusa.org/find-hostels/california · **$**

The HI name guarantees an affordable, well-run, and clean hostel. There are private rooms and shared-dorm options as well as comfortable common spaces. Its central location, between the Tenderloin and Union Square, means it is extra convenient for exploring the city on foot.

The North Shoreline

Samesun Hostel

F2 **1475 Lombard St** **samesun.com/samesun-san-francisco-hostel · $**

Enjoy sweeping views of the Golden Gate Bridge from the windows of this colorful hostel. The many room options range from private doubles to six-person dorms, and its free on-site parking is a rarity in the city. With the owners' handy tips for the area's best food, drink, and activities, Samesun is both a practical and friendly stay.

Kimpton Alton

F1 **2700 Jones St** **altonhotelsf.com · $$**

The Kimpton Alton is in the heart of Fisherman's Wharf, offering direct access to all of the area's delights, from top-notch sourdough to the sea lion colony at PIER 39. But you don't even have to go that far to have fun: the hotel has weekly DJ sets, poetry readings, and an award-winning Filipino restaurant, ABACÁ, on site. After a busy day, you can relax easily in the hotel's stylish rooms.

Fairmont Heritage Place

F1 **500 North Point St** **fairmont.com/ghirardelli-san-francisco · $$$**

Have you ever dreamt of living inside a chocolate factory? If so, a stay at the Fairmont Heritage Place will make these dreams come true. This all-suite hotel occupies the former Ghiradelli chocolate factory, and the current Ghirardelli Chocolate and Ice Cream Shop is just around the corner. It's a great option for families or larger parties (and all lovers of chocolate) – the suites have one to three rooms and plenty of space.

Seaside Inn

F2 **1750 Lombard St** **sfseasideinn.com · $**

Tucked away from the noise of the street, this family-friendly inn is a welcome respite from the Marina District's hustle and bustle. The rooms are simple but spacious and there is free parking on site. Check the website for regular deals and special savings when booking.

Presidio Lodging

D2 **Presidio of San Francisco** **presidiolodging.com · $$–$$$**

Stay on the grounds of the Presidio, the 1500-acre national park at the foot of the Golden Gate Bridge. Choose between the Presidio Lodge, with cozy rooms and views of the bridge, or the Presidio Inn, former US army barracks converted into stylish suites. Perfect for those who want to spend time enjoying the Bay's natural beauty, there's a free shuttle bus to take you around the sights.

Central Neighborhoods

Hotel Kabuki

F3 **1625 Post St** **hyatt.com/jdv-by-hyatt/sfojd-jdv-hotel-kabuki · $$$**

Located in San Francisco's Japantown, Hotel Kabuki's rooms have a contemporary, Japan-inspired design with cool artwork and sleek dressings. The highlight of the hotel, though, is undoubtedly the Nari restaurant, a Michelin-starred, Thai-California fusion experience.

Chateau Tivoli B&B

E3 **1057 Steiner St** **chateautivoli.com · $$**

This charming Victorian B&B is lodged between the Fillmore District and the iconic Painted Ladies. Join the likes of past fan Mark Twain in enjoying the almost-unchanged 1892 interior. And make sure to indulge in the weekend champagne brunch or afternoon wine-and-cheese tasting.

Inn on Grove

F4 **465 Grove St** **innongrove.com · $**

Comfort and convenience are king at this renovated roadside motel in the trendy Hayes Valley. Its rooms are quiet, clean, and affordable, and the hotel itself is close to the sights of the Valley but not the noise of the Civic Center. There is free parking on site and free Wi-Fi throughout.

Beck's Motor Lodge
📍 F4 🏠 2222 Market St
🌐 bechsmotorlodge.com
· $$

This third-generation family-run motel is at the northeastern tip of the Castro and Duboce Triangle, doubling access to a bevy of restaurants and nightlife. Though prices have increased from its original charge of $5 a night in the 1950s, it is still a well-located, affordable option in the city with free parking.

The Hotel Castro
📍 E5 🏠 4230 18th St
🌐 thehotelcastro.com · $

A stylish and compact 12-room hotel in the heart of the Castro, a stay here really delivers bang for your buck. It has a rooftop patio with views of the city, and each room and mini-suite is adorned with a different photo mosaic of a San Francisco icon's face. The caveat is that you must be sure to book ahead since space is limited.

Southern Neighborhoods

Noe's Nest B&B
📍 F6 🏠 1257 Guerrero St
🌐 noesnest.com · $$

Noe's Nest is a Victorian B&B that has ultimate comfort as its goal: a hot breakfast buffet is served every day, the cozy garden is a perfect spot to relax, and the hotel is pet-friendly, so your furry loved ones can travel with you, too. The rooms are antiquated in style but perfectly suited to a good night's rest.

Inn San Francisco
📍 F5 🏠 943 S Van Ness Ave 🌐 innsf.com · $$$

If you've ever wondered what life is like in the city's sprawling Victorian mansions, look no further than the Inn. This B&B in the buzzy Mission District has an elegant English-style garden with a hot tub, a rooftop sundeck with incredible views of the sunset, and a breakfast buffet with homemade Irish soda bread. What more could you want?

Hotel VIA
📍 H3 🏠 138 King St
🌐 hotelviasf.com · $$$

A valuable addition to San Francisco's hotel scene, Hotel VIA was built with sports fans in mind. Right across from Oracle Park, where the San Francisco Giants baseball team plays, this hotel delivers on in-room comfort and event convenience. It's also walking distance from the Chase Center, home of the Golden State Warriors (men's) and Golden State Valkyries (women's) basketball teams.

LUMA Hotel
📍 H4 🏠 100 Channel St
🌐 lumahotels.com · $$

LUMA Hotel is a stylish and colorful hotel in the heart of Mission Bay. Steps from the Chase Center, it's a great choice for those attending a basketball game or an event at the nearby Convention Center, too. The hotel itself has Twyne Coffee Bar for your morning coffee, Bodega Cafe for your lunch sandwich, and the Cavaña restaurant come dinnertime – a handy trio of meal options right on your doorstep.

Oceanfront

Ocean Park Motel
📍 A6 🏠 2690 46th Ave
🌐 oceanparkmotel.com
· $$

Nearly 90 years old, this nautical-themed Art Deco building was San Francisco's first motel. It is run by the same family that opened it in 1937, who originally built it for tourists coming to see the then-newly finished Golden Gate Bridge. And visitors still flock to see the bridge and take in this Art Deco Society landmark building, with its porthole windows and yellow exterior. Conveniently located at the southern end of Ocean Beach, it is within short walking distance of the San Francisco Zoo, stroll-worthy Lake Merced, and locally popular shopping and dining destination Stonestown Galleria.

The Seascape Inn
📍 A5 🏠 4340 Judah St
🌐 seascapesf.com · $

This no-frills hotel has spacious, air-conditioned rooms with especially comfortable beds to ensure easy dreaming at night. Just steps from the Golden Gate Park and the N Judah Muni line, it's a great location to get around all the city's top sights. There is parking at the hotel, and special offers are available on the website.

Seal Rock Inn

Ⓠ A3 Ⓐ 545 Point Lobos Ave Ⓦ sealrockinn.com · $$

The furnishings and decor at the longstanding Seal Rock Inn might be a bit dated, but the rooms are comfortable and the location, unbeatable. Far from the hustle and bustle of Downtown, the Inn has ocean views thanks to its location right by the Sutro Baths ruins and Lands End park. As an added bonus, the Seal Rock Inn's on-site restaurant is styled as a Parisian bistro and serves breakfast and lunch.

My Rosegarden Guest Rooms

Ⓠ C3 Ⓐ 75 20th Ave Ⓦ my-rosegarden.com · $$$

The staff make you feel like one of the family in this beautiful bed and breakfast. The four guest rooms are individually decorated for a unique atmosphere, and the breakfast is a family affair, with home-cooked dishes and the B&B's famous Sourdough Waffles. The cozy common spaces are great for getting to know your fellow travelers or just relaxing with a book after sightseeing. A stay to write home about.

The Bay Area

Costanoa

Ⓐ 2001 Rossi Rd Ⓦ costanoa.com · $$

In the quaint coastal town of San Mateo, known for its artichoke bread and olallieberry pie, Costanoa offers versatile ways to unplug from city life. Visitors can choose between camping, glamping, or staying in the eco-lodge. Given its beautiful coastal location, there is easy hiking access directly from the grounds and close to the beach. Costanoa also welcomes the whole family to enjoy their stay, with an arts and crafts playground and plenty of activities organized by the hotel, from tours of the on-site goat farm to orienteering lessons.

West Cliff Inn

Ⓐ 174 W Cliff Dr Ⓦ westcliffinn.com · $$$

This cozy, modernized beachside Victorian inn is a luxury coastal stay. All bookings include a homemade breakfast with a rotating menu of the chef's signature entrees. There's also an afternoon wine hour with local wine and savory snacks, and bikes and beach gear to facilitate exploring the beaches of Monterey and the coastal paths around the property. And to top it all off, after a morning of cycling and beach-going, you can return to the hotel for freshly baked chocolate-chip cookies.

Green Gulch Guest House

Ⓐ 1601 Shoreline Hwy Ⓦ sfzc.org/practice-centers/green-gulch-farm/visits-stays · $

Located in the quiet of Muir Beach, the guest house of the San Francisco Zen Center offers tranquility via meditations, dharma talks, farm and garden walks, and three included vegetarian meals per day – with Green Gulch's famous breads. Guests are encouraged to gather in the skylit atrium to relax or get to know one another, and there is an outdoor sauna on the grounds as well. There are also a few rooms in the guest house that can accommodate families with children.

Claremont Club and Spa

Ⓐ 41 Tunnel Rd Ⓦ fairmont.com/claremont-berheley · $$$

This sprawling 22-acre Tudor Revival-style resort sits on the rolling hills between Berkeley, Oakland, and a beautiful regional preserve. Visitors can luxuriate in the spa, play tennis or pickleball, or go for a dip in one of the three heated outdoor pools. With a focus on wellbeing, there are plenty of ways to relax at this beautiful property; the rooms themselves come furnished with luxury bath products and leafy views of the surrounding preserve.

INDEX

157

ACKNOWLEDGMENTS

This edition updated by

Contributor Margot Seeto

Senior Editors Keith Drew, Alison McGill

Senior Designers Laura O'Brien, Stuti Tiwari

Project Editor Molly McCarthy

Project Art Editor Bineet Kaur

Editors Catrina Conway, Anuroop Sanwalia, Vineet Singh

Proofreader Ben Ffrancon Dowds

Indexer Rhiannon Thomas

Assistant Picture Research Administrator Samrajkumar S

Deputy Manager, Picture Research Virien Chopra

Rights and Permissions Specialist Priya Singh, Vagisha Pushp

Publishing Assistant Simona Velikova

Jacket Designers Bineet Kaur, Laura O'Brien

Jacket Picture Researcher Simona Velikova

Senior Cartographic Editors Subhashree Bharati, James Macdonald

Cartography Manager Suresh Kumar

Senior DTP Designer Tanveer Zaidi

DTP Designer Rohit Rojal

Pre-production Manager Balwant Singh

Image Retouching-Production Manager Pankaj Sharma

Production Controller Kariss Ainsworth

Deputy Managing Editor Dharini Garesh

Managing Editor Beverly Smart

Managing Art Editor Gemma Doyle

Senior Managing Art Editor Priyanka Thakur

Editorial Director Hollie Teague

Art Director Maxine Pedliham

Publishing Director Georgina Dee

DK would like to thank the following for their contribution to the previous editions: Amber Charmei, Hilary Bird, Sam Cook, Lauren Viera

The publisher would like to thank the following for their kind permission to reproduce their photographs:

Key: a-above; b-below/bottom; c-centre; f-far; l-left; r-right; t-top

A NOTE FROM DK

The rate at which the world is changing is constantly keeping the DK travel team on our toes. While we've worked hard to ensure that this edition of San Francisco is accurate and up-to-date, we know that opening hours alter, standards shift, prices fluctuate, places close and new ones pop up in their stead. So, if you notice we've got something wrong or left something out, we want to hear about it. Please get in touch at travelguides@dk.com

Within each Top 10 list in this book, no hierarchy of quality or popularity is implied. All 10 are, in the editor's opinion, of roughly equal merit.

First edition 2003

Published in Great Britain by Dorling
Kindersley Limited, DK, 20 Vauxhall Bridge Road,
London SW1V 2SA

The authorised representative in the EEA is
Dorling Kindersley Verlag GmbH. Arnulfstr.
124, 80636 Munich, Germany

Published in the United States by DK Publishing,
1745 Broadway, 20th Floor, New York, NY 10019, USA

The publishers cannot accept responsibility for any consequences
arising from the use of this book, nor for any material on third
party websites, and cannot guarantee that any website address in
this book will be a suitable source of travel information.

A CIP catalog record for this book
is available from the British Library.

A catalog record for this book is available
from the Library of Congress.

ISSN: 1479-344X
ISBN: 978 0 2417 3852 8

Printed and bound in China

www.dk.com

MIX
Paper | Supporting
responsible forestry
FSC™ C018179

This book was made with Forest
Stewardship Council™ certified
paper – one small step in DK's
commitment to a sustainable future.
Learn more at **www.dk.com/uk/
information/sustainability**